Success

COMES FROM YOU

Success Comes *from* Creating the Best Life for Yourself

Dr. Christina S. Rogers

Dear Readers

This book will help you embark on your life journey to discover and pursue your passion, goals, and dreams. The purpose of this book is to help you build self-confidence to achieve your goals. It'll help you create strategies to become successful as you plan for your future. The content provides you with techniques that will encourage you to look at your strengths and weaknesses as a leader and learn how to transform those weaknesses into strengths.

Before you can discover your aim and purpose in life, it is important to learn who you are as a person. Only then can you determine what you want to become in life and apply this 'self-knowledge' to any situation that you come across in life moving forward.

Success is what you create your path will be. Remove all negative energy in your life to create a clear path towards success.

Life will challenge you. You will run into roadblocks. You will make mistakes. Trust me, I did. And it helped me get through those obstacles to create best practices and refocus on what is important to me in my life. However, you can't let these setbacks stop you from accomplishing your goals. You have to learn how to navigate through those obstacles and reinforce them in a positive way. If you don't, those obstacles will end up hindering your progress in life and take you one step away from achieving success.

Remember, it is important to be open to new opportunities in life. *As the famous saying goes, opportunities seldom knock twice…sometimes you have to take two steps back before you can move forward.* To make sure that you don't end up missing out on great opportunities, learn to make good choices, feed yourself with knowledge, seek support when necessary and center yourself around positive like-minded people to help you grow as an individual.

In essence, it is an honor that you've allowed me to guide you through this journey of life. I cannot explain how grateful and humbled I am that you chose to read my book to help you towards your success. I hope with all my heart that this book inspires and motivates you to create the best life for yourself. And by the time you turn the last page, I hope that you've learned to deal with life in a slightly more confident and optimistic way... And don't forget.

Success comes from YOU.

Today's Message: *Take the First Step towards Success*

Surround yourself with people who want to see you elevate, who are like-minded people you trust, who will push you to do better, who you can learn from – *knowledge is key,* who believes in your dreams, goals, and aspirations, and who you admire that will help you reach higher towards your success.

Best Wishes,

Dr. Christina S. Rogers

Acknowledgement

When I think of the word acknowledgement, I think of my dimensions in life – my support system. It is almost impossible to write a book without acknowledging my support system who helped me through this journey. Without the constant support of my family, I may not have been able to successfully finish this book – let alone have it published.

I would like to acknowledge my husband and children for giving me the strength and wisdom to tackle anything that I set my mind to do. They know I am a go-getter and a firm believer of SUCCESS. I am so grateful to them for believing in my dreams and for all the encouragement they gave me to write this book.

Thank you! Not just for believing in my dreams but knowing that I could get the job done without any hesitation to make this book a reality. I am so blessed and thankful to have you all in my life. Together, we stand strong and humbled - united as one.

Love You ALL!

Blessings,

Dr. Christina S. Rogers

Table of Contents

Disclaimer

The complete ownership of this book belongs to its author. No part of this book can be reproduced or transmitted in any form, including print, electronic, scanning, photocopying, mechanical, or recording. If there must be such a need to reuse the content of this book, written permission from the author should be taken beforehand.

This publication is meant as a source of valuable information for the reader; however, it is not meant to substitute direct expert assistance. If such a level of assistance is required, the services of a competent professional should be sought.

Although the publisher and the author have made every effort to ensure that the information in this book was correct at press time and while this publication is designed to provide accurate information in regard to the subject matter covered, the publisher and the author assume no responsibility for errors, inaccuracies, omissions, or any other inconsistencies herein and hereby disclaim any liability to any party for any loss, damage, or disruption caused by errors or omissions, whether such errors or omissions result from negligence, accident, or any other cause.

Author Bio

Dr. Christina S. Rogers is a wife, mother, Founder/CEO, executive producer, educator, director, professor, author, and a leader/mentor who supports her community. Dr. Rogers lives in Southern California with her family. She enjoys reading, researching, planning events, listening to music, dancing, shopping, and learning new adventures in life to better herself and most of all spending quality time with her family and friends. She has made a commitment to advocate for people who need support and guidance in their life and is fully determined to help others find their true SUCCESS.

Helping others brings a sense of peace and fulfillment to Dr. Rogers. It gives her great joy to bring and share her experience, knowledge, and leadership skills to teach worldwide in universities, schools, seminars, workshops, conferences, lectures, community events, and non-profit organizations.

In addition to Dr. Rogers leadership skills, she is also highly educated. She has received her Doctorate Degree in Education with an emphasis in Organizational Leadership from Pepperdine University focused on underprivileged students in education. She received her Master of Arts degree in Sociology with a strong concentration in Social Work. She also received her Bachelor of Arts degree in Human Services and Associate of Arts degree in Interdisciplinary Studies. To add to Dr. Rogers many accomplishments, she has received numerous of awards, certificates, nominations, and recognition for her work.

Dr. Rogers is an extreme achiever. She is goal-oriented, self-confident, strong-minded, and determined with a winners' mentality to reach for SUCCESS. She is a true definition of a ROCKSTAR BOSS LADY who never gives up on her dreams.

Dr. Christina S. Rogers

Success-To-Do-List

Do you have a recipe for success? In this section you will find my "Success-To-Do-List" that will help you identify and prioritize your goals. With the Success-To-Do-List, you'll be able to focus on the key elements that will help you create your own successful lifestyle.

Success-To-Do-List:

See your Goals in front of You

Understand that you have the Power of your Success

Create a Positive Mindset

Clear out all Negativity in your Life

Establish your own Personal & Career Goals

Stay Focused and Motivated throughout your Journey

Show Yourself and the World that you can do It

Chapter 1
Learn Who You Are As A Person by Discovering Your True-Self

"To know thyself is the beginning of wisdom".

This wise quote is attributed to Socrates – one of the most important philosophers in history.

Learn who you are as a person by discovering your life purpose through your true self.

Who am I?

How well do I know myself? What do I want in life? How can I achieve them? These are common questions that everyone should ask themselves.

This seems like very simple questions to ask yourself but answering it can be very complex. Some people might answer, *"What do you mean? I know myself as well as possible?"* While others may start wondering how well they really know themselves. Either way, chances are that most people who actually attempt to answer the questions may come up with the wrong answer.

Before you can achieve any type of fulfillment in life, it is important to really get to know yourself. Learn who you are as a person. Because without being aware of yourself, *how would you even know that something is supposed to make you feel fulfilled?* Without knowing yourself, you may also never be able to become a better version of yourself. Therefore, it is important that we begin this journey by discovering ourselves.

Self-Knowledge of Who You Are

Self-knowledge is a component of self. It is a term used in the psychology language of understanding self "Who am I"? "What I'm like"? This concept will have you thinking for days, months or even years. Your self-knowledge will help you to determine which things are right for you and which aren't. Without knowing what you're looking for, how can you find the perfect career or education for yourself? Developing self-knowledge requires an understanding of both the past and present. A full understanding of your goals, motivations, strengths, and weaknesses will enable you to make choices that really suit you.

Another benefit of knowing yourself fully is that it can differentiate you from other people especially from those who are not in support of your dreams. Take a minute to ask yourself, WHY? Do they really care for me? Do they understand me as a person? How do you define yourself? Think about the things you like: Why do you like them? Where did your interest come from, and why do you like it so much? Try to think about these things and write them down "create a vision board". This will help you visualize your dreams and have a clear understanding of your vision for success.

By challenging yourself and trying new things in life, you can observe and learn how you behave in new situations. Reflect self-knowledge is about knowing and understanding yourself, which means that you know your preferences, strengths, and weaknesses. Although you know yourself better than anyone else, it is good to know what others think of you. You may say "I don't care what other people think of me" but in reality, you do. Don't underestimate the power of self-awareness. This will make decision making much easier as you continue to find yourself. It may take a while, but it is definitely worth the wait. Also, don't forget that people change throughout their lives: therefore, knowing yourself is a continuous process. Become your master besides the master of your choices.

The Most Important Relationship You Have

We go through a lot of relationships in our lifetime. Parents, siblings, friends, cousins, significant others, coworkers, classmates and so many others. Yet, the most important relationship that we have in our lives is with *ourselves*. Despite spending time with others, most people don't invest as much time in their relationship with themselves as compared to how much they invest in other peoples' relationships.

This is a mistake.

> *"I make mistakes, and I'm learning from them and I'm not afraid to make mistakes. I enhance mistakes, they make you who you are, I never been afraid to fall so I say all these things but know I'm getting tested".*
>
> ~Beyoncé Knowles

That isn't to say that you shouldn't invest enough time in building relationships with others. You should, and you will. However, without working on yourself and becoming aware of your inner working, most outside relationships you form won't have the depth and integrity that many healthy relationships need.

Getting to know yourself requires some patience and effort. There aren't any shortcuts.

Learning how to know yourself will certainly help clear out any confusion in your life.

In life, your relationship with yourself is fundamental as it lays the foundation for all your other relationships. As you develop your relationship with yourself, you will develop other relationships more effectively.

Trust is the foundation of a good relationship with yourself, just like any other. Having confidence in yourself begins with trusting your wisdom and knowledge. You must have self-confidence and be able to lead yourself. Here are a few self-reflect questions to think about:

Are you confident in your own character? Do you know yourself well? Can you describe how you think? For how long do you need to decide? Do you perform well under pressure? What makes you happy? How do you feel about yourself? What are you most proud of? Are you confident that you can achieve your goals in life?

Your relationship with yourself is a very important aspect of life because it is the foundation for all your other relationships that you build upon. If you have a good relationship with yourself, you are in a better position to lead others, rather at home, at work, at school or in your personal life. Maintaining a healthy relationship with yourself requires balance. Too much self-criticism prevents you from developing the confidence that you need to succeed. Remember, the foundation of any good relationship is part of trust. As you become wiser and more knowledgeable about yourself, you will begin to trust your own judgment. The more you love and appreciate yourself, the better you can love and appreciate others.

Before we can learn how to understand ourselves better, it is also important to be aware of what happens if we aren't in tune with ourselves. Without understanding ourselves, the following five effects are likely to occur:

1. As you've already learned, knowing oneself is an essential step for reaching greater levels of happiness and fulfillment. This means that a lack of self-knowledge will lead to you making mistakes that will pull you away from being truly happy and fulfilled. When you don't have knowledge of yourself, you leave yourself prone to having misguided goals and accidents that can ultimately affect your success.

2. Arguably the biggest and most consistent issue you'll face if you don't take out time to learn more about yourself is insecurity. Without developing a sense of self-knowledge, you won't have any internal values to guide you through life. This will lead to you constantly second-guessing your decisions and wondering if you're making a mistake. This can have a serious impact on your self-confidence and can make you feel insecure as you'll constantly compare yourself to others while trying to measure your success or failure.

3. If you aren't aware of what truly makes you happy, you'll start measuring your happiness through other people's goals and ambitions. You will end up making other people's goals *your goals*. This will lead you to make a decision that may seem good for the goals you've set out to achieve but will be bad for your internal peace and happiness in the long run.

4. Without really getting to know yourself, you won't be able to learn about your core beliefs, dreams, aspirations, emotions, feelings, thoughts, and wishes, as well as fears, resentments, frustrations, and guilt. All of these are fundamental to who we are as a human being. Without learning about these fundamentals, you won't be able to make choices that lead to your *own happiness*.
5. Ultimately, if you don't get to know yourself, you won't truly be able to enjoy your life to the fullest. You may end up achieving the goals you set out for but if they were not truly *yours* to begin with, what are the chances they'll make you feel happy and fulfilled?

As you can see, self-knowledge is a means for you to achieve a greater level of happiness and fulfillment. Without a sense of self-awareness, you'll end up having second thoughts about everything you do and being insecure about your choices. And without an internal set of values to live by, you'll always compare yourself to what others believe. All of this can be a formula for disaster when it comes to living your life.

Practical Steps You Can Take to Get to Know Yourself Better

The good news is that you don't have to suffer from all these issues. Researchers have discovered some scientific elements of personality traits that can help you understand yourself better.

It doesn't matter how self-aware you are at the moment. What matters is that you decide to learn more about yourself. And once you make that decision, you can use various methods to follow through with the decision.

There are five basic character traits that are common to all people, regardless of gender, age or ethnicity.

Openness___*I have excellent ideas*
Sensitivity__ *I get easily offended/hurt*
Extroversion__ *I have the personality of being an extrovert, social and outgoing*
Compatibility__ *I get along with people very well*
Neuroticism___ *I have anxiety attacks and get irritated easily*

Taking the right steps to understand your character traits as well as your core values and beliefs helps you optimize your behavior and have better interactions with people around you which puts you in a better position to ask for what you need.

Understanding yourself means recognizing the gaps between your aspirations and the way you actually live your life. Because it is only when you know yourself, you notice the difference between how you are acting and who you really want to be. Therefore, a major part of learning about yourself is recognizing the discrepancies between who you strive to become and what you would realistically accomplish if continuously living the exact same way.

However, there is one more aspect that is very important to discuss is: *trust*.

And know, this isn't talking about how much you trust your significant other or your loved ones; this is talking about trusting yourself.

You must be thinking, *"What is this person talking about? Do they have any credibility? Of course, I trust myself. I may not know myself that well, but I know that I can trust myself. That's not even a debate."*

It is understandable if any of these thoughts are crossing your mind right now. But it is important to really understand what *trusting yourself* means. The idea "you may not trust yourself fully" can be really astonishing but also true for more people than you'd expect.

A lot of people try to hide parts of themselves from themselves. These could be the flawed, unflattering, or unpleasant parts of oneself that one isn't entirely comfortable sharing with the world. However, instead of working on this issue or trying to embrace it, we try to pretend that these parts don't exist at all. And if you can't fully trust yourself, would you ever be able to truly trust someone else?

It takes guts to trust yourself and accept yourself for who you are. It's okay if you are still trying to grasp the concept of trusting yourself. As you move forward with these methods of getting to know yourself better, you'll continue to gain the knowledge that you need to better reflect on yourself.

15

Just remember that investing in your long-term happiness is the most important thing you can do to live a successful life.

The Power of Self-Knowledge

Dr. Tasha Eurich has made a career out of demonstrating the strong link between knowing yourself and how others perceive you.

According to Dr. Eurich, people who invest time in getting to know themselves have a lot of advantages over those who don't.

> They are better decision-makers.
> They have better relationships both personally and professionally.
> They are more likely to raise mature children.
> They become smarter, more capable students, and choose better careers.
> They are more creative, confident, and better communicators.
> They also tend to be more adaptable. Throughout the learning and understanding process of knowing yourself, they also learn about the underlying foundations of morality.

The first step towards self-discovery is to acknowledge that you don't know yourself. A personality quiz can help you discover if you have positive or negative traits. This can tell you a lot about a person's priorities in life and what they believe they are successful at.

You can learn more about yourself by answering the following personality questions. Going through the following questions can give you a better understanding of how to begin the process of self-awareness. However, it is important to remain hundred percent honest with yourself while you answer these questions. It can be tempting to slightly alter your answers to fit the 'what you want to be like' narrative. But it is crucial that you resist this temptation. Or else, you won't lead anywhere. This is where trusting yourself is really important.

Remember the whole point of this exercise is to understand where you are and where you want to be so that practical step can get you there. So, if you are dishonest about yourself, you'll likely never be able to discover your true personality.

As you become more aware of yourself, it will lead you to understand how you held yourself back for so long.

20 Self-Discovery Personality Questions to Ask Yourself – Crucial Part of your Growth

1. How do I define myself?
2. How would I best describe myself in three words?
3. What are the most important things in my life?
4. What values are important to me?
5. How would I describe my ideal life?
6. How can I love myself more daily?
7. Who is my role model?
8. What are the things that I'm most proud of?
9. What has allowed me to reach this far in life?
10. What makes me happy about my life?
11. What was the happiest period of my life?
12. What qualities about myself do I admire?
13. What is my greatest achievement?
14. Who knows me best?
15. What areas in my life that I can improve on?
16. What do I feel is missing in my life?
17. What makes me the happiest?
18. What would I like to change about myself?
19. What is stopping me from my dreams?
20. What is one greatest obstacle that I am facing?

Analyze Each Question

Now, don't just go through the questions like an exam paper that you need to pass a class. Instead, take your time to thoroughly understand each question. Think about it. Really think about it and let it resonate with you. However, don't just limit yourself to these questions. Your determination to learn about yourself should also include reading personal development books and trying to understand the truth about yourself, even if it's unpleasant.

Known to Thyself	Not Known to Thyself
Know of Thyself The things we know about ourselves and the things others know about us	**Blinded by Thyself** The things others know that we don't know about ourselves
Hidden by Thyself The things we know about ourselves no one else knows	**Unknown of Thyself** The things we and others don't know about us

You can become more influential by understanding yourself. Sit down and examine yourself for a couple of minutes before you act. Consider this as a valuable *exercise*.

Getting to know thyself means understanding **YOU**. It means identifying when you don't live up to your expectations. A person who knows themselves well has a greater sense of enthusiasm. Researchers have discovered that self-awareness is the number one predictor of leadership success. If you don't trust yourself enough to know who you are, then who can you trust?

Path to Self-Knowledge

The most important way to start dealing with any period of change is to be honest with yourself. You cannot make decisions based on what you think you should do to please others. And without knowing yourself, you cannot be honest with yourself. You need to know your values, what you need in life, and what abilities you have.

Who am I?

The answer to this question includes your appearance as well as the way you behave. The way you behave in various situations largely explains your identity as a person, especially when you have to face a terrible or challenging situation. This is because during these times, you can feel vulnerable, and your inner feelings and beliefs may be exposed.

Where am I?

This is a term you might use to question your place in life. Sometimes, we think we know which road we are on. Yet, when we encounter bumps in the road, we start to rethink whether we have ever been on the right track after all.

How would you describe yourself?
Evaluating yourself is always difficult, but if you can, it shows a high degree of self-confidence and self-awareness.

Keep in mind that although these "who I am" quizzes are fun exercises, they allow us to understand our personality. However, they are not scientific and do not guarantee absolute accuracy. If you participated in the above "who I am" quiz but still want to learn more about yourself, there are several ways to accomplish this.

1. Start Maintaining a Daily Diary

A good way to learn about yourself is to start a daily diary. Jotting down your thoughts and feelings on paper is a good way to clear your head. It provides you with a platform to not only vent but also allows you to look back and see what you have written later on. In fact, it is one of the easiest and most effective things you can start doing to improve your mental health and reap various other benefits. Yet, most people don't give this practice the attention that it deserves.

There are many interesting diary tips that can help you better understand yourself. Set some goals. Look at every part of your life and ask yourself various questions about it. Where do you want to be? Write down things that are important to you. Write down things that you wish didn't exist in your life. Write down everything that bothers you. Learning more about your own personal goals and setting them in a single, easily accessible place can help you learn a lot about yourself!

2. Practicing Mindfulness

Mindfulness is another essential component of getting to know yourself better. Being mindful about how we interact with the world can teach you a lot about yourself. However, we're frequently enmeshed in our thoughts as we go about our day, thinking more about what needs to be done more as compared to what we're doing at the moment.

How often do you rush out the door in the morning without paying a single thought to how you want your day to proceed? Before you know it, a random person will cut in front of you while you're trying to get your bagel, and suddenly, your entire day will be ruined. When you're not mindful, you give other people and situations beyond your control a lot of power over your mind. This can lead to you feeling frustrated and resentful over the most minor of inconveniences.

The good news is that you can break this pattern. Just starting by taking a few minutes out of each day to practice meditation can be very helpful in the long run. At the same time, it can help you focus on your inner thoughts and allow you to be more in line with how you'd like things to be. This can enable you to work towards making your inner aspirations a reality.

Making consistent positive changes to one's life, even if they're small, is what makes a person successful. A successful and happy lifestyle cannot be achieved overnight. It takes time and patience. But if you make small changes in the right direction every day, you may be able to reach your goals sooner than later.

If you give yourself the opportunity, finding out who you really are can be the biggest and most important adventure of your life. We all have an awful inner critic who makes us think all the wrong things about ourselves. Even though many of us walk around being oblivious to this inner voice, it can still greatly impact how we perceive ourselves. We mistakenly believe that self-knowledge is self-indulgence. Hence, we carry on most of our lives without ever asking the most important question of all: Who am I really?

To understand who we are and why we act in certain ways, we must know ourselves. The only way to truly know who you are and why you act the way you do is if you know your story. Knowing your own story can help you to uncover who you are as an individual. The willingness to accept the past and to uncover our own truth is an essential part of understanding ourselves and becoming who we want to be. The willingness to explore your histories may be one of the best things you can do to understand yourself better.

Researchers have shown that it's not just the things that happen to us that define who we are, but also how we perceive these things and make sense of them. Every action we take today may be influenced by unresolved traumas from the past.

To understand yourself, you must identify what you want. Understanding your needs and wants helps you see who you are and what matters to you. While this may sound simple, you will find that many of us are defending ourselves against our wants in varying degrees. We may feel guarded because we don't want to hurt ourselves. As a result, we feel alive and vulnerable in the world when we want.

How to Practice Self-Reflection

STOP: Step back from a particular situation or take a break from life in general.

LOOK: Identify and get perspective on what you observe.

LISTEN: Listen to your inner guide, the wisdom that emerges when you give it enough space and time.

ACT: Determine which steps you need to take moving forward to change or improve.

What to Reflect On

Aristotle, Socrates, and Pythagoras are among the ancient philosophers who emphasized the importance of gaining knowledge of oneself.

Self-Reflection consists of two major components.

Reflect on the Important Aspects of Your Life (relationships, home and family, career, health and well-being, finances, goals, spirituality, and personal growth).

Reflect on YOU (This includes who you are and what you want to achieve or be in life).

In my experience, doing a self-knowledge exercise is the best method to regain your sense of self whenever you feel lost, or things feel out of control. You can look through the journal and reconnect with your authentic self by writing, thinking, or meditating. Your conversation with yourself should be only with yourself. For your life to go as you wish, you need to become aware of yourself. You'll be happier if you do. Yet getting to know your inner self is a long-term process. The path to change can be difficult as it requires years of self-reflection, introspection, and in some cases, difficult conversations with people you affect directly or indirectly.

On your journey to learning who you are, you will grow more comfortable being your true self, transparent, and even vulnerable. In harmony with your unconscious or true self, you will create the best possible life for yourself.

Process of Self-Reflection

As you learn more about yourself, the self-knowledge you gain helps create immense clarity on the journey of your life. This means clarity in all aspects of your life, including character, abilities, feelings, and motivations, and enables you to design the right strategies for success throughout life.

Here's a simple truth: *The path to success is paved with self-knowledge.*

Because it is only when you're aware of yourself that you can make a life that is satisfying in every aspect – whether it comes to your personal or professional life. On the other hand, a lack of self-awareness and information can lead to distractions, delays, and even derailments in finding and achieving your ultimate goal and purpose in life. As you understand yourself better, it enables you to be more confident in approaching your goals, increasing your chances of success.

The Wheel of Life
Finding Balance in Your Life

When you have a lot on your plate, it is easy to get distracted and not pay attention to the important things in life. Drive and focus are necessary for success in order to achieve balance in your life.

The Wheel of Life® (or Life Wheel) can help in this situation. The "Wheel of Life" is often used by professional life coaches and trainers to help with personal growth. It helps assess what is out of balance in each area of your life. As a result, it allows you to identify areas that need more attention. Originally a concept from Buddhism, the modern "Wheel of

Life" was created by Paul Meyer – a pioneer of the field of life coaching and personal development. Using the "Wheel of Life" is a powerful tool because each area of your life is shown in a circle so you can observe the current state of your life.

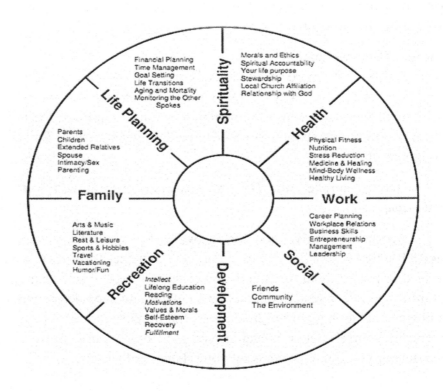

The Wheel of Life

The Wheel of Life allows you to reflect on aspects of your life you value that are important to you. Think about things that you will *start* to do to regain balance in your life. Think about things that you will *stop* doing, re-prioritize or delegate to help you balance your life out.

Small Exercise

Create your own "Wheel of Life". *(Use your computer, laptop, tablet, phone or draw it on a sheet of paper. etc.)*. When you are finished with creating your "Wheel of Life" as shown above, you will have a better outlook on the areas that are important to you in your life. You will be able to assess the amount of time you're devoting to each area – to balance your life out successfully. Remember to monitor your life balance as it changes over time as you mature.

Questions: *How will you improve your life balance? How will you maintain it based on what you have created in your Wheel of Life circle? Please share!*

Stages of Learning Who You Are
1. First impressions are everything. Practice good body language, smile and greet others with a firm handshake. Speak with confidence and make eye contact. This helps others to know that you are paying attention to their conversation.
2. Listen through interaction. Communication is an important part of a persons' behavior. YOU will learn about your characteristics through the person you are interacting with. This is a big part of your personal development on how you communicate with others.
3. Leave lasting memories of yourself. Your last impressions of memories, experiences, and connections will serve as a unique reflection of who you are and will allow others to become acquainted with you throughout your journey.

Happiness is Self-Knowledge
The keystone of happiness is self-knowledge. This is because, in order to be happy, you require emotional intelligence. Think about it: *Can you really be happy without a clear understanding of the type of person you are?* Only when you know who you are can you truly tap into your full potential, learn what you can accomplish, how you feel, and what motivates you.

Yet, trying to understand yourself can be a tricky challenge. Yes, you are the perceiver. And you've always told yourself that once you set your mind on something, you can achieve anything. However, in this scenario, you are also that object that is being perceived. This can turn the situation into a bit of a paradox, which isn't easy to solve.

As a result, it can be quite intimidating and stressful to actively seek self-knowledge. Because *who exactly are you seeking it from?* This can be absolutely true if you generally feel disconnected from yourself.

The good news is that no matter how self-aware you are at the moment; you can always begin your journey right where you are. And once you actively start seeking self-awareness, you'll start noticing how the journey gets easier along the way.

Fixed Mindset vs. Growth Mindset

FIXED MINDSET	GROWTH MINDSET
> Success comes from talent.	> Success comes from effort.
> I'm either smart or dumb.	> I can grow my intelligence.
> I don't like challenges.	> I embrace challenges as a chance to grow.
> Failure means I can't do it.	> Failure means I'm learning.
> Feedback is a personal attack.	> Feedback helps me grow.
> If you succeed, I feel threatened.	> If you succeed, I'm inspired.
> If something's too hard I give up.	> I keep trying even when I'm frustrated.

How to Become a Better Person: Self-Improvement?

Many people wonder if it's truly possible to become a better person as they get older. Yes, it's definitely is. There are always ways to improve yourself. However, you won't *automatically* become a better person as you grow older. If you want to better yourself, you need to make an active decision to do so and then work on it every single day of your life. While it may sound simple in theory, it raises more questions.

How can you become a better person?
Which is the easiest approach?
What are the most important aspects of yourself to work on?

These are some of the most important questions you need to ask yourself to become a better person. This includes considering both your own well-being as well as those around you.

We all experience anger at some point in our lives. It is pretty normal to have an angry reaction to various situations in life; it is human. However, uncontrolled anger can hurt your relationships and health and even make you less able to function at your peak. All of this can lead to more stress and more problems, making life more challenging and keeping you from becoming your best. For that reason, managing and eventually letting go of anger is essential to becoming a better person.

The bigger issue is that we don't always know how to let go of anger. Most of the time, people don't deal with anger in a healthy and constructive way. Besides, when you're mad, it always seems easier to lash out at someone or anything instead of taking a step back and reevaluating the situation. However, as difficult as it may sound, it is possible to do so.

In order to begin to deal with anger in your life, you need to learn how to recognize it and know what to do when you feel this emotion. If you notice that you feel unhappy and manage this emotion rather than deflecting it or acting out of anger, it will be easier to identify your anger.

Here's one thing you should always remember: *feeling angry and acting on that anger are two different things!*

Notice when you feel angry and why. Then, know your options. Besides focusing on your "anger triggers," you can also eliminate them. If, for example, you feel frustrated and angry when you have to rush, make more space in your schedule (even if that means saying "no" a little more), and look for ways to eliminate those triggers. To resolve an argument with an angry individual, you can limit their involvement in your life or talk things out with them. Trust me, you don't want this burden to keep you from living your best life.

Having a good understanding of yourself is the most valuable knowledge anyone can have. The journey to a fulfilled life begins with understanding who you are. This involves searching. You can't know what you want or who you are if you are disconnected from yourself. Ignoring yourself and your true intentions is the most damaging thing you can do. Knowing your true self will lead you to discovering who you really are on a personal level.

"You may not control all the events that happens to you, but you can decide not to be reduced by them".

~ Maya Angelou

Chapter 2
Want to Succeed in Life? Make Good Decisions

It can be quite scary to make decisions in life. There's always the fear of being wrong and not making the right decision at the right time. However, there's a bigger question at stake: *what drives your decisions?*

Decisions, decisions!

Our lives are full of them, from the small and ordinary things, like what we wear or what we eat, to life-changing ones, such as whether to marry, whom to marry, what work to do, or how to raise children. We are constantly faced with one decision after another.

We guard our right to choose carefully. It is the core of our personality: the definition of free will. Sometimes we make the wrong decision, which inevitably leads to unhappiness or regrets. Almost every moment of every day, we keep on making decisions. Sometimes, these decisions are small and irrelevant, and sometimes can change lives.

However, in the end, the results of your day, year, and entire life are mainly defined by the sum of the decisions, as well as the actions you take along the way. There is power in making a decision – even if you're not entirely sure whether it's the right decision. I assure you, once you understand the incredible impact of making a decision, you can truly start assessing your own decision in a powerful way.

The ability to make good decisions requires you to balance the seemingly antithetical forces of emotion and rationality. As individuals, we must be able to predict the future, assess current circumstances accurately, understand the thinking of others, and deal with uncertainty.

Decisions – we make decisions every day. With every decision we make – good or bad – our lives become a little more defined. Each decision we make ultimately shapes who we are as a person.

We all have the power to influence change. This power is from the choices we make. *"Tomorrow's blessings and opportunities depend on the choices we make today."* In our choices, we have the power to change our lives of those around us and the power to choose our destiny.

If you want to change your life and make better choices, start with a small step; today. Our destiny is influenced by the choices we make. How you perceive it can change your actions on it. And how you act can change your feelings.

When you change how you feel, think, and behave, your physical health also becomes better. Therefore, for a better you tomorrow, make better choices today. The power of your destiny is within you.

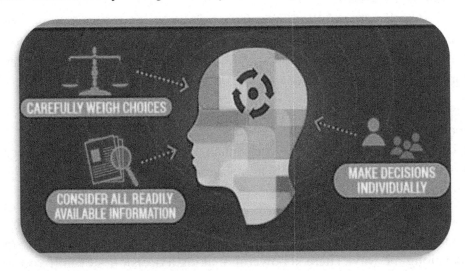

5 Steps to Good Decision Making

Every day we face situations in our lives that require us to make choices. Some of these choices are easy, and sometimes, some of them can be difficult. Simple decisions include what to eat, what movies to watch, or what TV shows to binge on. It seems that the most difficult decisions are those that require deeper thinking. Examples of difficult decisions include things like where to attend college, choosing the best career path, and/or whether starting a business or a family. These types of decisions are difficult because they are life-changing decisions; they shape who we are and your future.

When it comes to decision making, you can choose from various steps. But when making good decisions, there are really five steps that should be carefully thought out.

First Step: Identify Your Goal

An effective decision-making strategy is to always keep your eye on the goal. The process of identifying the purpose of your decision simply involves asking yourself: *what exactly is the problem you desire to solve? Why does this problem need to be solved?*

Understanding what you value most will guide you to make the best decisions for your future. If you understand the reason why you have made a particular decision, you will be better equipped to stand by it, as well as to defend it.

Before making a decision – especially those that affect you in the long run – make sure to weigh your pros and cons.

Second Step: Gather Necessary Information

Before making decisions, it is important to gather all the necessary information that can directly impact the problem. By doing so, you will have a better idea of what needs to be accomplished in order to resolve the issue, and you will generate ideas for possible solutions.

A good idea when gathering information is to list all possible choices, even those that initially seem silly or unrealistic. You should always ask the opinions of others you trust or speak with experts or professionals when weighing all your options for a final decision. Making the right decision will be easier if you gather as many resources as possible to streamline your decision-making.

Third Step: Assess the Consequences

Assessing the consequences of your final decision can be just as important as step one. It will allow you to see how your final decision will affect you and/or others. You will be analyzing the outcome of your decision in this step. What impact will it have on you now? What effect will it have on your future?

It is an important step since it allows you to evaluate the pros and cons of the different options. Also, you want to feel confident and comfortable about all the options you have available to you and the possible outcomes.

Fourth Step: Make Your Final Decision

Once you have identified your goals, gathered all the necessary information, and assessed the consequences, you are ready to make your final decision. To be successful in this step, it's important to understand that some people are very anxious. This is a situation where you'll need to trust yourself.

You need to be aware of how this makes you feel, even though you may still be indecisive about your final decision. Ask yourself, does it feel right? And does this decision work best for you right now and in the future? When you answer those questions back directly, you should feel good about the result at the end of the process.

Fifth Step: Evaluate Your Decision

After making your final decision and taking the necessary steps to put it into action, it is important to evaluate the decision and the steps you have taken to ensure that it is effective.

The final step in the process of determining the most appropriate decision-making approach is just as important as the first one, if not more so, because it further enhances your ability to make decisions for future problems. This step allows you to seek new information and make some changes along the way.

Remember, this step will require some patience and it can also encourage perseverance. Why? Because it may take some time for final results to appear. Having the awareness that if the first decision doesn't work, you may need to go back to step 2 and choose another option.

When problems occur, always be aware of the outcome. These five steps can help simplify and reform the decision-making process in a more effective way.

In summary, we all have to make many decisions throughout our daily lives. There are some decisions you can make quickly, while others will need to think about more deeply before coming to a final decision... And that's okay. Remember, you make your own decisions and don't look for other peoples' approval for everything. You own you!

31

In situations with many steps, people tend to forget steps or misconceive the order in which the steps should be taken. Practicing the techniques, you learn in order to improve your decision-making skills is a very important part of building your power. By following these five steps, you will be on the right path towards making good decisions for yourself.

Key Takeaways

Decision making involves choosing between alternative actions as well as inaction.

There are both automatic, programmed decisions, as well as non-programmed decisions.

Several different structures lead to structured decision-making processes, including rational thinking, bounded reasoning, intuitive reasoning, and creative reasoning.

All of these strategies can be useful depending on the circumstances and the problem at hand.

Exercises

How do you determine whether your decision will be successful or unsuccessful? How long before we know if a decision is successful or not?

Research has shown that over half of the decisions made within an organization fail by individuals. Does this surprise you? Why or why not?

Have you used the information in a decision-making process? What was your experience with the process?

Describe a decision you made where you satisfied your needs. Were you pleased with the outcome? Why or why not?

Describe a situation where you made a mistake during the decision-making process. What led you to realize that you had a poor decision? How did you overcome it?

Reflect on Your Decisions Today	
Write down two decisions you have made today. Why did you make these decisions?	
My Decision	**Why I Made This Decision**

Reflect on Your Decisions this Week	
Write down two decisions you have made this week. Why did you make these decisions?	
My Decision	**Why I Made This Decision**

Reflect on Your Decisions this Month	
Write down two decisions you have made this month. Why did you make these decisions?	
My Decision	**Why I Made This Decision**

Reflect on Your Decisions this Year	
Write down two decisions you have made this year. Why did you make these decisions?	
My Decision	**Why I Made This Decision**

"If people are doubting how far you can go, go so far that you can't hear them anymore".

~Michele Ruiz

Chapter 3
Understanding the Importance of Time Management & Setting SMART Goals

To achieve any type of success in life, it is important to focus on two things: time management and setting goals.

Time Management

Effective task and time management involves three key processes:

1. Itemizing – listing all key tasks that needs to be accomplished along the path towards that goal.
2. Prioritizing – attacking tasks in the order that it was received.
3. Scheduling – deciding when tasks are to be started and completed.

It is highly recommended to divide your tasks into A * B * and * C tasks. See example below:

A. Essential Tasks-- what should be done now.
B. Important Tasks-- what should be done soon.
C. Optional Tasks-- what could or might be done if there's time remaining after you've completed the more important tasks on the A and B list.

In an effective time, management plan, work and play are balanced to encourage our mental and physical wellness. An effective time management plan can function as a stress-management plan. There should be a way to reduce stress and learn more while still making time for other important things. Remember, maintaining a healthy balance in your life can go a long way.

The best time management plans are those that become action plans. A time management plan turns into an ongoing action plan by:

1. Introducing what we plan to do,
2. Analyzing the results of our actual efforts, and
3. Bringing our intentions and actions closer together.

By setting Smart Goals you can:

Become more effective

Achieve better results

Drive yourself harder

Experience greater satisfaction and pride in your accomplishments

Become more self-confident

Reduce stress and anxiety

Avoid thinking and acting in ways that cause unhappiness

Concentrate better

Focus on the work that you have done and what you can do

Procrastination

Effective time management can be impacted by procrastination or postponing what should be done right now. Procrastination is not synonymous with laziness. Below are six styles of procrastination, along with suggestions on how to overcome them.

Procrastinator	Type of Description	What Can You Do?
Perfectionist	Perfectionists - don't want to fail themselves or others. Your focus is always on getting things right. Consequently, you delay getting anything done by doing more than you need to.	Change your mindset from everything must be perfect to everything will be as good as it can be. Be able to distinguish between what is practical and what is ideal. However, this does not mean you have to settle for inferior work. It simply means you should allow yourself some leeway. Don't put pressure on yourself without reason.
Dreamer	You have big ideas, but you don't follow through on them.	Putting plans ahead of dreams will help you achieve them. Create action steps and implement them one at a time.
Worrier	You avoid taking risks. You avoid committing to something that may be risky rather than doing something different or challenging.	Don't be afraid to assert yourself. Associate with positive people who will help you see your talents. Try a little calculated risk (nothing foolish) every week to get used to stretching yourself.
Crisis Maker	You put off doing what you are supposed to until the last minute. Projects are more successful if there is more pressure attached to them. Unfortunately, as more projects stack up, you are not able to complete them satisfactorily.	Establish deadlines that are not too close to the actual deadline-maybe two or three days in advance.
Defier	You don't see why your time should be affected by other people's demands, like	Refocus. Ask yourself, "What can I do?" and "What do I need to do?" rather than

	class attendance. It is possible for you to choose a low priority task (for example, washing dishes instead of reading or studying), instead of one of higher priority.	"Why do I have to do what they want me to do?" You made a choice to come to school.
Overdoer	If you don't know how to say no, you take on too much, run out of time, and turn in half-done or unsatisfactory work. You may be able to accomplish some tasks well, but eventually, you run out of energy and crash.	Reevaluate your goals. Be careful not to overextend yourself; make sure that your goals are being met before taking on too much. In order to be self-centered, one·must be willing to help others.

Schedule Your Time

Arrange as much time as possible. Don't prepare in the morning without planning how to spend the day.

Try to set aside at least one day or a few hours in your schedule – *Protect this time.*

Keep track of what you need to do. Use the calendar for daily tasks: classes, homework, meals, etc. Create project diagrams for long-term commitments with deadlines. Planning in these ways can help you stay organized.

Keep your email inbox empty. Delete, reply to, or move messages to folders while reading them.

Limit your time on the internet and social media. We all know that a few minutes of strolling down…can turn into a few hours in a blink of an eye.

What Kind of Goals Should I Set?

There is no right answer to this question. Choosing goals that are important to you personally is essential. You should set goals in different areas of your life. You should set your goals based on your desires - not what your family or friends want for you. Consider the following topics while trying to set your goals:

Education - Is there any knowledge you want to acquire in particular? What level of education or skills do you need to obtain to achieve other goals?

Career - What level or type of career do you want to reach? What do you want to achieve within your career?

Financial - How much do you want to earn? How much do you want to save, by what age?

Family - How do you want your relationships to be? How do you want others to see you?

Artistic - What do you want to create? How do you want to create things?

Attitude - Is any part of your mindset holding you back? Is there any part of the way you behave that should be improved or changed?

Physical - What kind of physical lifestyle do you want to lead? How do you want to feel about yourself (both physically/emotionally)?

Pleasure - How do you want to enjoy yourself? How do you want to feel at the end of each day? What can you do each day to improve your emotional well-being?

Public Service - Do you want to make the world a better place? Who do you want to help? How do you want to help?

As people change, acquire new knowledge and skills, and discover new talents, their goals can change by the following:

Step 1 - Goals: It's what you want to do now or later.

Step 2 - Responsibilities (Priorities): It's what you have to do and what's important to you. When discovering your priorities, ask yourself, why is it important to me? How will my set of priorities be beneficial towards my future goals?

Step 3 - Balancing: Work and Play.

We all have obligations and responsibilities (school, work, business, family, and/or friends), so how do we balance everything? According to your goals and priorities, *realistically* plan your week in advance to balance out successfully.

Step 4 - Planning: How do I balance my priorities and goals?

Use a planner or calendar. Once you put your goals on paper or on your device, you should feel more obligated or reminded of what you need to do to reach your goals. Check often so that you know when important deadlines are and how to plan your week accordingly.

Step 5 - Re-evaluation: Why is it a process?

Okay, so you planned out your week but still didn't have enough time to do everything. Now what?

Re-evaluating is important since it keeps you in the constant process of improving and revising your use of time. Your priorities will change, so you must be flexible in your use of time management skills.

A Goal without a Plan is just a Wish. You need a clear direction in life...having a clear direction can make your path much profound and successful.

~Dr. Christina S. Rogers

TIPS on Goal Setting

How Many Goals should I have at once?

    Have no more than 5 active goals at a time.

    Prioritize your goals. Organize them from 1 – 5.

    Empower Yourself with Goals - When you achieve your goals, you feel great about yourself!

    Setting goals is a powerful activity. It gives you focus. When times get tough, it keeps you going. When you feel afraid, you can focus on goals, not on the current dilemma or yourself.

Why Set Goals?

    You put yourself in control, not others.

    Goals keep you from being too hard on yourself.

    Goals keep you motivated.

    Goals make you better at performance in all areas of life (personal, academic, career, etc.)

Goals Should Be…

    Long term 1 year to 5 years or longer. Depending on your timeline.

    You might call these focused dreams. (Remember, they have a plan and a deadline.)

    Short term – Take the long-term goals and break them down into shorter steps: 1 – 6 months. Objectives – Take the short-term goals and break them down into steps again: 1 week to 1 month.

Elements of Goals

    Specific: Describe the goal in detail.

    Measurable: Days, hours, weeks, months, years, 2 times a week for 3 hours, etc.

    Realistic: Can you really accomplish this goal?

    Completion Time: Include completion dates. (You can always revise these later).

    Who/what will help you: Include what assistance you will use?

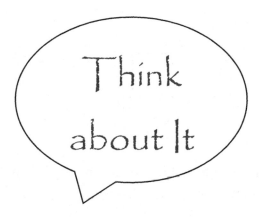

Think about It

Practice Writing Your Goals:

Setting Smart Goals

Part 1: Write Down 3 Goals:

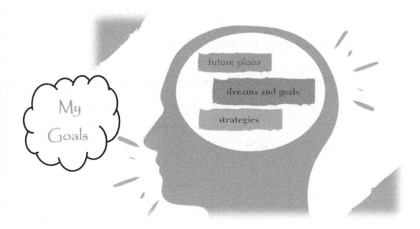

1. _____

2. _____

3. _____

Pick one goal from above:

Part 2: Break your goals into smaller steps – remember these are measurable and attainable.

Steps	Time Needed	Deadline

Part 3: What are your resources in achieving this goal?

_____

_____

_____

What obstacles might get in the way?

_____

_____

_____

What will you do to overcome these obstacles?

_____

_____

_____

Part 4: How will you know you have achieved this goal? What will it look like and what will it feel like?

_____

_____

_____

_____

As you learn the significance of time management and goal setting, you may be able to determine what road to take for yourself. You will learn to master time management and setting goals from the approaches, ideas, and techniques offered in this chapter. In order to maximize your personal and professional success, you need to acquire and practice time management skills and setting SMART goals for yourself. Setting goals for the year and working hard to achieve them will help you succeed. When you don't set any goals for yourself, how will you know if you are where you want to be in life? As you proceed on to the next chapter, keep that in mind.

"Are you committed to your goals? Because without commitment nothing happens".

                                                              ~T. D. Jakes

Chapter 4
Strive for Excellence: You Have the POWER

"Strive for excellence in everything you do"

Ask yourself:

- Why do we strive for excellence?
- How can you achieve excellence without power?
- What can you do **today** to better yourself for tomorrow?

There is no such thing as perfection. No matter how much you try to achieve perfection, you'll always end up finding some imperfections and flaws. And that's perfectly fine. Humans are meant to be flawed.

However, something beautiful can come out of striving for perfection. The effort you put into improving yourself develops your energy level and enables you to achieve more.

"Perfection is not attainable, but if we chase perfection, we can catch excellence."

~Vince Lombardi

Implementing the following ideas can help you take a step closer to perfection.

Define Your Values

In order to make the right choices in life, you need to know what truly matters to you; you need to understand your core values. You can start by making a list of things that you value. These could be anything from goals, traits, and habits to skills, causes, social and environmental issues, etc.

You can also include observations regarding how you and others live according to your core values. Make sure to revisit your value list often to ensure you are focusing your efforts on what is most important to you.

Listen with an Open Mind

If you stay fixated on yourself, you will likely not get an opportunity to grow or prosper. Discover others' stories by listening to them.

Try to hear what the other person is saying, sensing his/her emotions and reactions as you offer your advice and similar experience. As a result, you will gain a deeper understanding of other people's needs and values. You may be surprised at how much you can learn from other people around you.

Generally, people just want to do their very best.

Yet, at what point do we decide that we are close to achieving excellence? And more importantly, at what point do we realize that we are crossing the line of too much perfection?

Striving for perfection is completely different from striving for excellence. When you strive for excellence, you can really feel motivated and inspired. On the other hand, striving for perfection may cause you to feel demotivated when you don't get the exact results you want.

Excellence means *'to excel'*. It is a quality that is exceptional or exceptionally good. To pursue excellence, you must constantly evaluate where you are and what you need to do to improve. By striving for perfection, you aim to achieve something so good that it can't be improved or enhanced anymore. This way, you run the risk of probably never reaching it.

If you think about it, every single one of us is always striving for excellence on a daily basis. You are concentrating most of your efforts on things that work well. And when one thing works out – or doesn't work out – you move on to the next thing you can do. Because we all desire to do better, we all want to succeed.

If you want to achieve excellence in your personal or professional life, here are some suggestions to consider:

8 Ways to Strive for Excellence

1. Know that you are strong and capable of doing anything you set your mind to do.
2. Be proud of yourself and your accomplishments.
3. Connect with others who value your talents.
4. Develop new skills as you strive to be the best you can be. Be kind to others and show compassion.
5. Regardless of what challenges may come your way, do your best to tackle them. Be authentic and give yourself permission to be you.
6. Make yourself a priority and put your own needs ahead of everything.
7. Break out of your comfort zone. Be open-minded and try new things.
8. Accept the challenges that are thrown at you and thrive to be a phenomenal leader. Learn from your mistakes and failures in life.

Humanity Means Living Our Greatest Potentials

As humans, we always dream of success and growth. It is the basic human instinct to want to become a better person.

However, it is sometimes difficult for us to live up to our full potential. No one is perfect. We struggle to achieve growth and excellence on a personal, professional, and academic level. There are many of us who know what it takes to grow and succeed. The majority of us are not aware of how to take the right steps to ensure that one is successful and is achieving excellence at every level.

The irony is that many of us desire excellence, yet we aren't always willing to strive for excellence. You see excellence requires effort. It requires you to be on your feet consistently until you have achieved everything you set out for. Most people aren't too keen on doing the hard work – they want quick results.

In reality, that's not how things work in real life. No matter how hard you try, it will take some time to get to where you want to be in life. If you're truly passionate about something, you will have to put in time, effort, and patience. Only then can you achieve excellence in life.

Remember, excellence should be the top priority of our lives in order to grow and achieve excellence. And it can be achieved by always striving to do better.

People who do not strive for excellence have a difficult time in their life. They may not feel satisfied with their lives and would always feel like *something is missing*.

In contrast, people who constantly strive for excellence feel happier and satisfied inside, and contribute positively to others, so excellence refers to a state of exceeding some standards. As we grow and develop our abilities to do better and better in all facets of our lives, achieving personal excellence becomes a lifelong process.

In terms of personal excellence, it is the journey of positive development beyond oneself and the step-by-step process of improving oneself in all aspects of one's life. Even though the process is challenging and requires patience, it can contribute to a happy and successful life for people who want it.

To achieve personal excellence, you must continuously improve your performance in all areas of your life – family, education, career, finances, relationships, etc. However, being successful in every aspect of your life does not mean you have to be perfect. This process involves improving oneself and continuously doing so in all aspects of life.

As individuals, we tend to deal with challenges around us, such as work, family, friends, careers, etc., without considering the root causes. The only way to grow and succeed is to master ourselves.

A key to understanding the concept of personal excellence is to consider the following:

Vision and Life Purpose
Self-Control
Determination
Empowerment
Patient
Self-Belief
Resilience

Perseverance
Adaptability
Growth Mindset

These concepts will guide you on how you can gain personal excellence. However, you will also find other ways and tools for achieving personal excellence, which is also great sources of learning. An individual who is committed to personal excellence makes every effort to make themselves perform better and better, to maximize all of their talents and abilities at a level greater than usual; and to focus on their overall well-being and high level of personal growth.

Those who have achieved excellence in their personal lives enjoy fulfilling relationships, have successful careers, and are well respected around the world. It manifests as self-defined and self-valued achievement reflecting one's best efforts. The willingness to win, the desire to succeed, and the desire to reach one's full potential are the keys to unlocking personal excellence. To succeed in this instant, you need to believe in yourself, set realistic yet high goals, keep learning, and challenge yourself to expand your skill set.

Personal excellence is built on understanding yourself, exploring your mind, thoughts, and attitudes, and understanding how you respond to challenges. Spend time with yourself to explore and fully reflect on who you are to strive for excellence.

Every person has a unique skill set that varies from one to another. When achieving personal excellence, your growth mindset is very important because it gives you the right direction on how to utilize your strongest abilities to perform better and learn what skills you are best at by using them to improve yourself on a continuous basis.

The best way to be happy is to do what you love the most, enjoy it as much as you can. Being aware of what you enjoy in your life is the key to achieving personal excellence. The best way to evaluate yourself is to understand what you are good at and what you enjoy doing to excel in every platform in your life. The famous saying "Action speaks louder than words" is true.

Re-evaluate and re-strategize yourself to perform at the highest level to strive for excellence!

~Dr. Christina S. Rogers

Try this simple exercise: Say each sentence without stopping...Go!

- *I must strive to do my best at all times.*
- *I will aim for excellence to achieve my goals.*
- *I will work hard to find what makes me happy in life.*
- *I will not let anyone get in the way of me achieving my goals.*
- *I will trust myself to strive for success.*
- *I will believe in myself before believing in others.*
- *I will have a firm determination and mindset to WIN.*
- *I will always have power over my life.*

Having read each sentence, take a moment to reflect: how do you feel at the moment?

You Have the POWER

When you have your mindset on what you want, you are challenged to take power over your life. By embracing your own power, you are accepting that you have a definite role to play in your own destiny. To find and become your true self, it is essential that you harness your own personal power.

The concept of personal power is built around self-assertion as well as a natural, healthy desire for love, satisfaction, and meaning, says Dr. Robert Firestone. Knowing our personal power means we will accept that we have a profound influence on our lives. We create the world we live in. To create a better world means shifting our outlook, feeling empowered, and rejecting a victimized point of view.

Dr. Firestone pointed out "The 6 Aspects of Being an Adult" that you must experience:

1. Your emotions but make rational decisions when it comes to your actions.
2. Identify and achieve objectives by formulating goals and taking action.
3. Instead of being passive and dependent, be proactive and assertive.
4. Ensure that all relationships are equal.
5. Open your mind to new ideas and accept constructive criticism.
6. You have full control over every aspect of your conscious existence.

Why Should You Strive for Excellence Not Perfection?

"I am careful not to confuse excellence with perfection. Excellence I can reach for; perfection is God's business."

~Michael J. Fox

The ability to achieve excellence is relatively easy when compared with attaining perfection. As you become more focused on achieving perfection, the unbalanced pressure will precipitate mistakes. In contrast, if you are striving for excellence, you are relaxed as when you realize mistakes are always okay, you will be able to improve yourself in the process.

Although high standards may be challenging, they are attainable. Our efforts, practice, and perseverance can help us achieve them. However, it is futile to strive for perfection. In spite of this, perfectionists strive to meet impossibly high standards.

Having impossible standards for yourself only adds stress to your life. You can't live up to these standards you've created for yourself without feeling demoralized. No matter how much you accomplish, you constantly feel like a failure. Similarly, setting impossible standards for others, such as your family or co-workers, can create disputes. It can lead to nagging, frustration, and arguing that destroys your relationships and leaves them demoralized.

Excellence means being satisfied with your work. Mistakes don't define you, but they do teach you. Not only do you enjoy the process, but also the outcome. As individuals, we remain flexible and can adjust our standards and goals as needed. In addition to our accomplishments, when we strive for excellence rather than perfection, we stay in balance; we value self-care, as well as our accomplishments.

People should always strive for excellence and make sure that they prove their worth, even if they feel like they're never good enough. People often attempt to prove their worth to others, whether it's their parents, friends, significant other, or themselves. I personally strive to prove my value to myself. It has been known since ancient Greece that excellence is something to strive toward. In ancient Greece, the pursuit of excellence came to be known by a word: *Areté*. The word means to "strive for excellence".

Perfectionists Perceive Mistakes as Failures

People who strive for excellence accept mistakes as inevitable and value what they learn from them. They don't let their mistakes define them. Perfectionists view mistakes as an indication of their inadequacy or inferiority. Their expectation is to know everything, to outperform everyone, to always do or say the right thing, to be above reproach, and to never disappoint anyone. Besides being unrealistic, this is a heavy load to carry.

Perfectionists must have everything on point – there is no room for mistakes. It is not only their ambition to be the best, but also their attitude that anything less than perfect is unacceptable to them. While excellence is the belief that mistakes can never be made or imperfections can never appear, perfectionism is an expectation that we will never make mistakes or have any imperfections. Excellence is more forgiving than perfectionism, as it allows a little room for mistakes and imperfections.

It is mainly a matter of our attitude toward mistakes or flaws that differentiates excellence from perfectionism. Overgeneralizing mistakes and shortcomings are a common tendency for perfectionists. When we make one mistake, we see ourselves as failures or inferiors. The thinking error keeps perfectionists focused on the negatives, incapable of seeing the positive aspects of mistakes and imperfections when there are many benefits to learning from mistakes and embracing our imperfections.

Expecting perfection will lead to disappointment inevitably. Despite being smart or working hard, everyone makes mistakes. Instead, we must strive for excellence to keep us going. In order to attain excellence, the person must strive high but offer self-forgiveness for mistakes made and things not yet learned.

When you expect yourself to do the impossible, you are constantly disappointed. When you criticize yourself harshly, you are more harshly criticized than your actual mistakes. Despite your success, you will never believe you are good enough.

The Perfectionist Values the Outcome over the Process
Pursuing excellence or high standards means valuing the process, in addition to the outcome. As we grow, we also build memories, fun experiences, and relationships along the way. In addition to valuing the process, we are also better able to cope with life's ups and downs since we recognize the outcome doesn't always reveal our skill, intelligence, or efforts.

Achieving goals is particularly not pleasing enough for perfectionists because they are results-focused rather than process-focused. As a result, they only focus on what went wrong and cannot appreciate doing things imperfectly. The perfectionist mindset can also serve to justify a success at any cost. If we think like this, we do not appreciate the lessons learned from mistakes and we don't appreciate learning, growing, and striving for excellence.

The following are three quotes that Dr. Rogers follows to sustain a successful lifestyle:

- STRIVE *to achieve the best foundation in life.*
- EXCELLENCE *comes from by you putting in the work in life.*
- POWER *yourself to make you better mentally, physically, and spiritually.*

Strive for Excellence Activities

Exercise No. 1: Identify the three essential quotes that will guide you through a successful lifestyle.

These can be any quotes or statements. It can be a quote by Aristotle or a lyric from your favorite pop song. Or something your professor/teacher said that motivated you. The point of this exercise is that it must speak to **you**. Something that inspires you to get out of bed and work towards your goals to create a successful lifestyle.

Below are quotes that will help you get started:

1. Optimism is the one quality more associated with success and happiness than any other. ~Brian Tracy
2. If the plan doesn't work, change the plan, but never the goal. ~Anonymous
3. Opportunities don't just happen. For them to become a reality, you must work hard every day. ~Dr. Christina S. Rogers
4. You will succeed because most people are not dedicated as you are. ~Shahir Zag
5. The grass is greener where you water it. ~Neil Barringham

Exercise No. 2: Answer to following 16 WHAT QUESTIONS:

1. What are you hoping to accomplish, acquire, and do?
2. What do you wish to see happen?
3. What would you like to do better?
4. What would you like to have more time for?
5. What would you like to have more money for?
6. What do you consider to be the most important thing in life?
7. What made you angry recently?
8. What have you complained about?
9. What person would you like to get along with better?
10. What would you like to get others to do?
11. What changes will you have to make?
12. What are you wasting your time on?
13. What is too complicated?
14. What are your life's obstacles?

15.   What are some ways you are inefficient?

16.   What things would you like to be better at?

Ask yourself these questions? Write them down. Discuss your answers with someone you trust.

Everyone strives for excellence or strive to be perfect. Right? We all want to have a good job, a big house, great family, and friends and perhaps even the opportunity to travel the world. But ask yourself, why do you want all these things? If you live your life to make others proud of you and not for your enjoyment, you will miss out on what GOD has in store for you. The focus should be on living a lifestyle that you are proud of. By implementing this simple philosophy will put you in a better place. It will allow you to see the brighter side of life. You learn to appreciate your effort and celebrate the little victories in life especially when you start thinking of perfection as a journey and progress as the goal, you will learn substantially more. I've learned that people who strive for excellence develop a learning mindset. They do not let failures get them down. In fact, they view failures as an opportunity to learn and improve...they always strive for excellence. Needless to say, this changes their life in a positive way that gives more *POWER* to make a difference.

"Don't settle for average. Bring your best to the moment. Then, whether it fails or succeeds, at least you know you gave all you had. We need to live the best that's in us."

~Angela Bassett

Chapter 5
Motivation is the Key Factor to Success

Without motivation, it is almost impossible to strive for success and maintain happiness.

Anyone who is motivated to accomplish something will be more committed to the task and will put all their efforts into it. It may seem easy to stay motivated when you're committed. However, when you feel demotivated, you must remind yourself the importance of commitment to your success.

Motivation leads to self-development. Once you reach your personal goals, you will be more motivated and inspired to work even harder to achieve even more. It's important to remember that success is only the vision, and happiness is what matters the most. Without happiness, there would be no motivation to succeed.

Take a moment to reflect:

Do you think motivation is important for success and happiness?

What Motivates You?

Most people have some motivation in them, but not always for the same reasons. It is important to recognize and understand that each of us have different motivators. This enables us to understand that just because something that motivates you does not motivate another person does not mean that they are not motivated to succeed.

Everyone experiences moments of motivation at some point in their lives. There are two basic motivators:

1. Obtaining, needing, or wanting something or
2. Fear of losing someone or something

These motivators cause people to take certain actions in order to either win or avoid losing something.

Here Are 12 Ways To Motivate Yourself

Get a good start to your day by using one or more of these ideas.

1. Know What Motivates You

   Motivating yourself takes reflection and some thought. You need to know what motivates you in order to be motivated. Once you have answered these questions, you can use the successful strategies listed below to recreate your mojo.

   - What gets me motivated?
   - What reduces or stops my motivation?
   - What reminders do I need to stay motivated?
   - What can I do to increase my motivation?

For maximum motivation, you need to identify what motivates you, as well as what demotivates you.

2. Don't stress over the Small Things

   Certain things are beyond your control. Don't let your frustrations demotivate you, even if there are many things you find irritating every day. Keep your focus on what matters to you to avoid negative feelings.

3. Identify your 'Zone' (and training yourself to stay in it)

   When you're in the zone, you produce your best work. Put yourself in a position to do your best work by creating a supportive environment. Is music necessary for you? Make a playlist of motivational music with your headphones. I personally find this to be very motivating to me.

4. Check off items on your To-Do List

   In addition to keeping, you focused on your most important priorities, creating a to-do list makes you feel good when you cross off items and move on to the next item on your list.

5. Surround Yourself With Productive People

   By associating yourself with productive individuals, you can learn from their methods and pick up on their healthy productivity habits. Positive individuals tend to be more productive which may motivate you to work harder and accomplish more.

6. When to Ask For Feedback

Feedback is needed sometimes but not all the time. In case you lack motivation, asking for feedback on something that you did well can provide you with the boost of confidence that you need to master your craft.

7. Reward Yourself

Set yourself up for success by rewarding yourself when you complete dreaded tasks. It may motivate you to drive through and complete a task faster when you know you'll receive a reward at the end. You can reward yourself with downtime, an outing or anything else you find enjoyable.

8. Enjoy Yourself More

You can keep yourself motivated by making work more fun. Even though you think it's simple, often you get sidetracked by your work. You already enjoy certain aspects of your day. Make time for these activities.

9. Log Off

Set a cutoff time for yourself if you're feeling stressed and feel like you cannot escape work. As you are making your way home or when you wake up in the morning, checking your email won't alleviate feeling overwhelmed. Make an agreement with yourself not to check your email during non-working hours. It will help you accomplish other things that matters the most too.

10. Discover New Things

Self-education is the best way to learn something. Gaining new skills can increase your productivity, boost your self-esteem, and help motivate you to a new height.

11. Give Yourself A Break

Motivating yourself to get your best work done may not always be a good idea when you lack motivation. Take your time and make sure you are being productive at all times.

12. Create an Idea Folder

The list you create can serve as your go-to spot for inspiration regardless of whether it is a book you want to read or a side project you want to tackle. This will help you stay organized through your thought process as well.

Tips to Increase Motivation

Surround Yourself with Positive Motivating People

Your surroundings influence your personality. When it comes to learning how to be motivated, the first step might be to observe others. Look for positivity in people. It is important to consider the impact that they will have on you. Eventually, you will begin to see how these positive individuals motivate themselves. This will help you motivate yourself as well.

Use Positive Affirmations to Motivate Yourself

Using positive affirmations to encourage yourself are statements like, "I set achievable goals," "I achieve my goals," or "I want to succeed". These types of statements will encourage you to turn from negative to positive and provide the motivation you will need to succeed.

Learn to Understand What Motivates You

Each person is different. For some people, money motivates them, while for others, helping others is a strong motivator. Identify what genuinely motivates you.

Why Motivation?

Why do you think motivation is the reason you don't succeed? I could have been promoted if I was more motivated." Or, "If I was motivated enough, I could have received an A." You now know that "lack of motivation" isn't an excuse since we can take steps to discover what motivates us.

Self-motivation is a person's ability to achieve goals despite inevitable obstacles and problems. Unlike extrinsic motivation, which is activated by other people, self-motivation is within us, and depends on whether we see the problem as a failure or a challenge.

Self-motivation begins in childhood with the development of early work habits, postponing present gratification for long-term gains, rational goal setting and a strong desire to achieve them. Sometimes, focusing on

57

role models will solve your biggest self-motivation problem which can be another step toward success.

Self-motivation happens spontaneously. If our goal is too important or too tempting for us, we will react. For example, if we are very hungry, thirsty, or cold, we will immediately be prompted to take action to relieve this unpleasant feeling.

There is a story about the famous philosopher Socrates, who was once asked to explain what success is. To demonstrate this, he asked the young man to follow him down the river and dive into the water. The young man tried hard to get some air, and at last, Socrates let him go. He explained to this young man that just as his greatest desire was to get some fresh air, he should also desire success. Thus, the history of self-indulgence is difficult and predictable because not all of us will respond to the same stimuli in the same way.

Generally speaking, we all have great potential to achieve many goals, but success depends on how important they are to us or how much we really care about them. Our self-motivation is greatly influenced by our attitudes and beliefs about ourselves and the world around us.

This secret power was in the mind of Steve Jobs when he pursued success. He was a workaholic and tough when it came to business. Even when a customer opens a box and finds the product in it, he or she gathers a team of people to research the feeling of excitement. He relied heavily on emotion and self-motivation. In his mind, time was also important.

Time is temporary and cannot be saved for later use. So, love your living days as if they were the last. Yes, self-motivation is the key to success. I believe that everyone is always motivated by themselves. But whenever you do something that someone else dreams of, motivation will always be a challenge.

There are times when encouraging others is more effective than motivating yourself. You may be surprised to learn that other motivational activities are self-motivating too.

How Meditation Increases Focus & Motivation

Meditation is why people are able to focus on life; it keeps us motivated towards our craft. If you want to achieve greatness, you need to stop asking for permission. This is why motivation is important in life because it stops asking questions and aligns you to work towards your goals.

Motivation is the defining factor that turns a good thought into immediate action. It turns a good idea into a business and can positively impact the world around you. Without motivation, you can't achieve anything.

Motivation can also help you personally to be the best you can be. This can have a positive effect on your confidence, relationships, and the community you live in.

Just think about how you position yourself in life.

Six Reasons Why Motivation is so Essential in the Journey of Life

1. Clarifying Your Goal Through Motivation

Motivated individuals possess a desire to change their lives and are motivated by what they must do. Motivation pushes you towards your goal because of a desire for change. You can become motivated by knowing exactly what you are striving for and how you will get there.

2. Priorities in Life are Set by Motivation

Motivating yourself is one way to prioritize your life once you understand what your goals are. If your goal is to write a book, you need to put aside time each week so that you can dedicate yourself to this daily task. Motivation helps you focus your attention and make an effort to get to the point where your goal is reached.

3. Motivation Pushes Through Setbacks

There is always going to be a setback on the road to success. I believe that in order to reach your dreams there is no such thing as the dream route. Having setbacks can cause you to doubt whether your goal is worthwhile, but motivation makes you stronger and gives you the courage to carry on.

If reality asks you to give up, your motivation won't let you.

4. Fighting Fear with Motivation

It is so common to fear failure that it can literally prevent you from taking action. In order to avoid fear, you must be motivated to do it. Motivation tells fear that it will not matter what you feel or think. Motivated individuals grasp the concept of visualization and can move beyond their fears. It is always motivation that allows you to see the bigger picture.

5. The Power of Motivation Build Self-Confidence

Motivation to succeed leads to confidence when small steps are taken to reach that goal. A sense of accomplishment comes from pushing through setbacks and fear; this builds inner self-confidence for trying something new.

Motivational people will also have a couple of projects ongoing because they have already faced obstacles and seen positive results which gives them the motivation to try new things and start new projects.

6. Motivation Inspires Others

Motivation is an attractive characteristic that can inspire others to accomplish things in their own lives. Whenever you are around a self-motivated person, you feel as if you can achieve anything because of their positivity and can-do attitude.

You can elevate your own motivation levels by seeking out motivated individuals. Motivation is a muscle. If you read biographies, attend trainings, or listen to motivational speakers, you will learn more from their own successes as they build you up.

Key Success Motivators

Motivating yourself is one of the keys to success. However, you may not be completely aware of what motivates you at the beginning of your career. In another case, you might believe that you are motivated by one thing, such as money, while your true motivation is having free time versus having money.

When the aim of your leadership is to inspire, you must find and identify the key success motivators for the people who will be helping you fulfill your goals. When you use these ideals to motivate people, you will effectively drive them to work harder because the reward is intrinsically higher.

Here are the top ways to measure success and how you can use them to motivate yourself:

Enjoyment and Ambition:

Enjoyment and ambition can also be powerful motivators for some people. Success can make some people feel narcissistic in their motivation. When people always striving to be the best or improving upon things from the past can use this to their advantage.

Provide for Others:

Many people are also motivated by the desire to provide for others. This doesn't have to be in a charitable manner - it could revolve around creating jobs or the ability to pay others to live comfortably. Motivating people with this approach might be difficult for a leader, but it may help you find the ideal project for an individual.

Enjoy time to Yourself:

Reward Yourself. Take vacations or make free time for yourself may be the biggest success motivator for you. Working hard and playing hard goes hand-in-hand but remember you must get the job done and don't waste time doing it.

3 Keys To Self-Motivation that will Build You Up

1. Taking Charge of Your Life:

Never stop improving yourself. You must always be striving for improvement. You should always know that putting time and effort into YOU is the greatest gift you could give yourself. No matter where you're at in life, you can use your potential to transform your situation by focusing on developing yourself.

2. Don't Settle For Less:

The majority of people settle. What have you settled for lately? In life, settlements are becoming more common amongst people. Rather than settling for what we really deserve, we settle for less. The fact that we don't feel good about it doesn't stop us from taking advantage of it.

3. Embrace Life with Energy & Passion:
    The life you lead is either a happy one or a sad one. It is either you are going the right way, or else you are in the wrong direction. You want to smile, you want to be happy, you want to be free, well in this case you have a lot to be thankful for with this kind of mindset. Your energy and passion will tell it all.

How to Motivate Yourself

Tasks Can Be Broken Down Into Small Steps:
    When it comes to motivating yourself, there is a reason so many people recommend using this method – because sometimes the simplest things can be the most effective things.

    Put together a work plan that details each step you'll need to take to make your work plan happen. Let's put everything else aside and focus on the steps you're currently working on. As soon as you start to flow, it may just become easier to complete the next task.

Develop an Attitude of Gratitude:
    Getting motivated can be difficult if you find yourself stuck in a rut. Before you try to motivate yourself, take a step back and try to appreciate how you feel. Feeling appreciated will make it easier for you to remain motivated. It is almost impossible to feel low and grateful at the same time. Practicing gratitude is one of the quickest ways to feel good about yourself.

    Write down three things you're grateful for in order to practice gratitude. It could be anything - your morning cup of coffee, your pet, or even your comfortable chair.

    To find motivation on a daily basis, you should make this a part of your daily routine.

Treat Yourself with Kindness:
    It's easy to beat yourself up when you procrastinate or make a mistake. Many people think that they internalize negative self-talk.

    If you catch yourself doing this, pause and try speaking kindly to yourself instead. You wouldn't speak that way to someone else, so why would you do it to yourself? Kindness comes from within.

Remember that you are a human being with true inherent value. Return gently to the task at hand after you have taken a moment to reflect.

Constructive Feedback is the Best

When you realize a mistake that you have made and finally come to your senses after procrastinating for a period of time, your opportunity to learn and improve is golden.

Do you ever wonder why you made a mistake? What can you do to avoid making the same mistake again?

You will transform mistakes into opportunities if you do this and act on what you learn.

It is important to accept that we may not always make the right decision…mistakes happen, and that failure is not the opposite of success, but rather a necessary part of success.

You Can't Change Your Future If You Don't Change...Imagine that!

It's easy to motivate yourself if you imagine the life you'll have if you don't stay motivated: Instead of focusing on the change you want, imagine your life if you don't stay motivated.

Ask yourself, *'How will the world be one year from now, five years from now, ten years from now?'*

"You can either experience the pain of discipline or the pain of regret. The choices are yours."

~Dr. Christina S. Rogers

Reflect on How Far You've Come

Do you take the time to pause, reflect, and appreciate the progress you've made?

Many people don't give themselves enough credit for all their growth over the years. Let's take a few minutes: Close your eyes and relive your successes in life, no matter how small. Keep yourself motivated by doing this activity often. It will help you rethink and plan for your bigger successors in life. When you become your own successor, you continuously grow and transform your concepts stronger to build your foundation of success.

Take Time to Remind Yourself "Why"

Motivation comes from doing what we are passionate about.

Write down three reasons why you want to be motivated to do things. What are your goals: a better body, a better education, saving money, or starting a business?

Why? Try to come up with as many answers as you can until you find those that sustain you.

Eliminate Distractions

You must avoid distractions if you want to stay focused. Motivating yourself begins with eliminating distractions.

You can eliminate distractions by disconnecting from people for a little while, shutting off your phone, closing your door, turning off your music or TV, or whatever you think may help. Remind yourself that you're not punishing yourself but simply concentrating on your goals. Consider what you truly want long-term.

Don't Be Afraid to Ask for Help

When you're having difficulty motivating yourself, talk to a friend or family member who can give you encouragement. Keeping them up to date on your progress is a good way to hold you accountable.

Making your goals more concrete by talking about them with someone else helps the connection feel real. You may be more likely to follow through if someone is checking in on your progress.

Get Inspired by Others Who Motivate You

Many inspiring people can motivate you to succeed. Can you think of anyone you find inspiring? A teacher, musician, entrepreneur, or politician?

Don't Forget your Power and Potential

You are powerful, and you have enormous potential. The main reason people give up their power is that they believe they don't have it.

So, please, dig deep and connect with your inner power and potential - imagine what you could achieve. "You can do it."

"Success isn't about how your life looks to others. It's about how it feels to you. We realized that being successful isn't about being impressive, it's about being inspired".

~Michelle Obama

Chapter 6
How to Be a Good Leader:
Learning Leadership Strategies the BOSS Way

Doing it the Boss Way...

Are you a Leader or a Boss?

Despite their similar dictionary definitions, there is a crucial difference between bosses and leaders in the business world.

It is possible to be a boss and a leader at the same time?

If you are wondering how to be both a good boss and a good leader, there is good news - you can do both! By focusing on your leadership skills, you will be able to achieve the goals that the boss in you sets, while also having the authority of a leader.

As a leader, one of the most powerful strategies is to use a coaching approach. Leaders and bosses must first understand what the emotional triad is and how it influences the state of mind and behavior of an individual.

There are three factors that control someone's' emotions:
Focus
Language
Physiology

A leader is the one who influences and changes each of these forces within themselves and others in order to achieve desired outcomes, inspire people, and make them enjoy the journey. You want to learn about the differences between boss and leader - and how you can lead even if you have no title.

Is there a secret to becoming a great leader?

Having the right principles and support will help anyone grow into an effective leader. Many great leaders began as ordinary people and had to learn how to lead.

To go from good to great, you must start by asking yourself:

- *Is my best effort sincere and genuine?*
- *What is the most important area for improvement?*
- *What are some ways that I can set a more meaningful vision that inspires people?*
- *How can I better understand the needs and wants of the people around me?*
- *Most importantly, what do people expect from me?*

As you ponder upon these questions, you'll gain valuable insights into what steps you need to take.

Are You a Boss or a Leader?

Being a good leader may also mean being a good boss. But you can't be a good boss if you're not a good leader. If your entire focus is on gaining profits for yourself, you won't be a great boss or an effective leader. Instead, your focus should be on the people.

Being a leader means showing people how to act in order to constantly improve themselves. It is important to understand that you are leading individual human beings, not a group of pre-programmed robots. This means you need to understand that each individual is different and work accordingly. At the same time, it is also essential to identify your own needs as you recognize who you are.

Make an effort to notice the impact you have made as you become more aware of yourself as a Boss or Leader.

Leaders Lead You, Bosses Push You

Leaders guide and motivate people to move together as one. When a leader inspires their team, the team follows their example. People are influenced by great leaders. The best leaders are skilled in their fields and have a knack for generating new ideas.

Bosses push and order their subordinates while hiding behind them. It is the bosses who expect their subordinates to work without guidance and achieve results.

Why is Leadership Important?

In some way or another, you could say that we're all leaders. Whether you're running a family, a house, a team, a department, or a

67

company, you are likely leading something. When it comes to guiding your family, team, classmates, department, or corporation for a very long time, it is important to become the leader they need.

If you are serious about becoming a great leader, you must acknowledge that leading others is a huge responsibility and that you will need to overcome various challenges in the process. Therefore, you have to prepare yourself for the obstacles you'll encounter. Not only do you need to prepare yourself for the challenges, but you also must be ready to face the consequences.

What Characteristics Make A Great Leader?
Despite the diversity of leadership styles, there are some basic characteristics that are shared by all leaders.

To understand them, here are a few examples:
Good listeners: Lead with listening instead of talking: leaders know that listening is the key to success in communication, which is why they prioritize listening over talking.
Constant learners: A leader who is always learning - whether from books, courses, or mentors - is someone who seeks to learn from other people's experiences.
Leadership through Service: Good leaders understand that influencing people begins by helping them achieve what they want; they serve others and ask for what they need.
Healthy Living: The greatest leaders in the world understand the importance of taking care of their bodies and well-being to remain productive.
Taking Accountability: Leadership is taking responsibility for the decisions they make and owning the results.
Focused: A leader who is focused understands what is critically important and will focus their efforts on it.
Compassionate and Empathetic: Effective leaders are compassionate and empathetic and strive to help people in specific ways.

This is not an exhaustive list of all the characteristics of great leaders, but it covers some of the most crucial ones.

Steps to Becoming a Great Leader:

At this point, you're likely asking yourself how to become a great leader. Leaders are like parents. There is no step-by-step method that works for every situation.

Let's discuss a few tips that can help you get off to a great start.

Leaders who lead themselves always succeed. Knowing yourself is the first step towards managing yourself. Leadership involves understanding who you are, along with where you are most open to learning and growing. Start by knowing your strengths and weaknesses. Take time to assess your strengths and determine where you can be the most valuable.

- *What are your methods of learning?*
- *What is your communication style?*
- *Would you rather listen, write, or express yourself through action?*
- *Which kind of group settings work best for you?*
- *What is better, cohesion or tension?*

Ponder upon these questions for a while before trying to come to a conclusion. The thing is that the first *answer* you come up with may not be 100% accurate. Therefore, it is necessary to think about these questions for a bit longer to really become aware of yourself. If it helps, write these questions down or discuss them with someone you can trust. Do whatever allow you to feel more enlightened because as you grow and learn about yourself, the answers to these questions may change so keep revisiting these questions as life goes on.

Are you Ready to Become a Great Leader?

Having leadership skills isn't just about giving orders, getting compliance, or even building close relationships with people. A great leader is someone who helps his or her team grow and achieve its full potential by building a strong culture. The aim is not to make them feel obligated but to support your cause because they are as committed to it as you are.

You're right. It'll be hard – you got this!

There is no doubt that you'll have to deal with many obstacles and challenges along the way.

The cost of getting ahead will be high. You will have to make many sacrifices. So, if you do it right at the beginning, I am confident that everything will be worth wild at the end.

What Makes a Good Leader?
There are 9 Essential Traits to Master

A strong leader is more important than ever in today's fast-paced, technology-driven world. *What makes an effective leader? What are the benefits of strong leadership in your life?*

1. Leaders are clear in their communication. Good communication is key to being a successful leader. Whether it is in a face-to-face interview or an e-mail, good leaders say what they mean and mean what they say. A passive-aggressive attitude is not a trait of a good leader, nor do they hesitate to confront challenges directly.
2. Leaders are passionate about what they do. Good leaders aren't afraid to show their passion to inspire people further. It is still possible to be an effective leader even if your personal and professional interests aren't aligned. Take time to figure out what you enjoy most about your work and develop a passion for it - you may even find that you put yourself in a position to have greater workplace satisfaction.
3. Leaders aren't concerned about their popularity. When your first concern is whether everyone likes you, you may be less effective. It doesn't matter if you give tough criticism or point out an unethical practice; learning how to be a good leader involves doing or saying things that are best for your team, your group, or your organization, regardless of its consequences.
4. Leaders keep their minds open to new ideas. Being open to new ideas is another quality of a good leader. Leadership is about being flexible and adaptable instead of resisting change. Regardless of their own opinions, they're open to different perspectives. Remember, your aim isn't to order people around. Instead, you want to grow and improve together.

5. Leaders are part of their team. Leaders may answer to higher-ups, but they also know their primary mission is to ensure their team has the resources to perform their jobs as effectively and efficiently as possible and the support they need to thrive in whatever role they have.

6. Leaders are encouraging and positive. Having a good leader is uplifting. They praise their team's successful work and are willing to coach and train them if necessary. A good leader helps people blossom in both good and bad times by encouraging them to do their very best. Don't be rude or unnecessarily stubborn with your team. Despite being tough, we are all humans. Sometimes cutting someone some slack if they are going through a difficult time, such as a painful break-up or the loss of a relative, isn't a big deal.

7. Leaders treat others with respect. Leaders can earn respect by conducting themselves ethically and modeling what they expect of their team. Demonstrate that you understand where you are going and that you know your team is doing the right thing with you. Those who are good leaders treat others just as they want to be treated. When leaders lead by example, their environment is often strengthened. Be sincere as well. To build a peaceful atmosphere within your team, you must ensure they feel confident that unpleasant surprises are unlikely.

8. Leaders cultivate relationships with other people. A good leader is able to establish and maintain productive relationships. Win the trust of others. Those who feel that their leaders are trustworthy will become engaged and loyal. Getting involved in your team's everyday work problems is the first and most important aspect of building trust. Be sure to pay attention to those who are behind everyone else and make sure they understand their tasks. It is also important to understand what they are like outside of work. However, don't overdo it – nobody likes bosses who are too intrusive. Effective leaders recognize the importance of collaboration with others and actively seek out them.

9. Leaders serve as an example; they keep on moving forward. Leadership is full of examples, and set the right ones is an essential part of their effectiveness. Good leaders are ready to do anything

their team requests from them, from providing extra hours on big projects to treating others with kindness and dignity. Leaders never stop learning. One of the most important characteristics of good leaders is that they are continuous learners. The first step they take is to educate themselves, whether it is through formal education or through the day-to-day tasks they perform. Every good leader wants to learn more.

Transform from Boss to Leader

As you progress from being a "boss" to a "leader", the personal development experience can be incredibly challenging and rewarding. As a leader, you will help your team produce effective and lasting results, and their performance will be consistently outstanding. They'll have increased productivity at work, as well as more fulfillment in their personal lives.

Developing your role from boss to leader is a kind and a service act you can perform for your fellow human beings – and for yourself as well. Leading others will make your life more fulfilling and less stressful.

Leadership is ultimately determined by the culture promoted by a supervisor. Leadership culture can be seen when an individual truly has leadership qualities rather than just the title. The organization includes all levels of leadership opportunities.

When there is a true leader in the organization, people are inspired, accountable, engaged, and feel ownership over their work. People who feel like they are being ordered around by their boss or doing other people tasks generally are disengaged. It can be frustrating for a boss to want the team to do the work a certain way, leaving them to wait in the wings until they are told how to get started. Leading requires an understanding of what it means to lead and analyze how you demonstrate your leadership capabilities.

A good leader conducts their decision-making process based on the best interests of the team as well as the company. Listening leaders grow to influence and impact, while those who neglect to listen to their team will struggle with disengaged people who won't listen. A leader who wants to be listened to should practice listening to their people under them. Whether you see yourself as a boss or a leader, the key to your success is if others know what they can always expect from you.

After reading the following comparisons, consider your own actions to determine which leader you are:

Bosses Oversee, Leaders Lead

As a boss, you are responsible for making sure that your staff follows the rules of the organization, but a leader will empower others with the freedom to come up with their own creative solutions. As bosses, we give orders to tell others what to do, but as leaders, we can motivate others to make smart choices and encourage future growth.

Leaders Inspire, Bosses Explain

A boss makes sure that the team understand the work. In contrast, the team needs a leader for support and guidance. A leader is more than just a boss...a good leader inspires and encourages people to do their best. Success requires passion. Without the will to succeed, staff will not be as motivated to do their best. As a leader, never underestimate the importance of the work they do.

Bosses Discipline, Leaders Mentor

As a boss, your attitude toward mistakes reveals what you are like. Great leaders realize that both encouragement and mentor-ship help others achieve success. While bosses are more likely to use rewards and punishment systems to promote good behavior, great leaders understand the power of encouragement and mentoring. Among the qualities of a good leader is the ability to involve others to reach a common goal. In place of attacking skill gaps, guide participants through their shortcomings and build their confidence to pursue new opportunities.

Leaders Delegate Authority, Bosses Delegate Tasks

Bosses follow protocol meticulously to achieve the objectives of their organization. They think for the short term, delegate tasks to their subordinates, and tend to micromanage. Bosses have the success of telling people what to do and are concerned about doing it right. Leaders have the results of enabling their teams to figure out what to do in order to come up with the best results and are concerned about doing the things that would lead to the highest rewards.

Bosses are above Teams, Leaders are Part of Teams

Being a good boss or leader means maintaining a good working relationship with your team. Consider their needs and create an environment that fosters open communication.

Loyalty and authenticity are requisites of good leaders. Your team looks up to you. If you lack passion or motivation, odds are your team will lack these too. Don't be afraid to be yourself - communicate with your teams' emotions and authentic self.

What Makes a Great Boss?

Leaders guide their team through motivation and encouragement. Coaches guide people by example and practice. A great boss views themselves and their role as both leadership and coaching. A great boss will understand that success in coaching comes from managing control - that fine line between too much and too little - and being enough of a presence to help.

Great bosses create an environment that promotes integrity, trust, and respect, as well as one that encourages feedback, innovation, and creativity.

Six Things Leaders Must Do If They Want To Succeed

If you want to become an effective boss, it is important to shift your way. As a leader, you want to become an effective boss. In order to succeed in a leadership role, alter the way you think and act in the following 6 areas:

1. Mindset: Gather resources to help you lead effectively now that you're leading others as well as yourself.
2. Relationships: You should aim to take on the role of "boss" instead of simply "friend" while working.
3. Attitude: You will need to delegate tasks instead of trying to handle everything yourself.
4. Perspective: See the whole picture, not just a one-sided picture.
5. Focus: Do what is right rather than what is comfortable or convenient for you.
6. Skill set: Learn new skills so that you can manage your team successfully.

Leader vs Boss: A Leader Listens, But a Boss Transforms

Leaders are capable of disrupting patterns to shift focus, eliminate limiting beliefs, and inspire internalized changes. This is accomplished through active listening. When other people speak, they don't just listen. They strive to understand what they're saying. Whenever they read between the lines, they listen with full attention and make eye contact.

By knowing how to accomplish this, strong leaders can successfully interrupt others' habits of thinking, believing, or acting. Once they become more aware of these patterns, they can choose to pause, refocus, and change their beliefs and behaviors to be more empowered.

Leaders also strive to bring changes to their organizations. Their response doesn't end at hearing complaints - they act on them. Their resourcefulness has enabled them to access the tools they need for their team.

"Your work is going to fill a large part of your life, and the only way to be truly satisfied is to do what you believe is great work. And the only way to do great work is to love what you do. If you haven't found it yet, keep looking. Don't settle. As with all matters of the heart, you'll know when you find it."

~Steve Jobs

Chapter 7
Create Boundaries by Removing Bad Energy: Positive Vibes ONLY

How to Create Healthy Boundaries to Protect Your Energy

Setting Boundaries for Negative People in Your Life!!!

Have you ever dreaded seeing a person because they were always negative, and you always felt drained every time you interacted with them?

Is there ever a time when you dread opening up an email from a certain person because he/she just seem to be negative all the time and you always feel drained after responding to their email?

Do you ever feel exhausted looking at a number calling or texting you that you dread answering too or what about reading their long text messages? Or how about when someone hurts your feelings by saying negative things about you? Do you reply negatively? The answer is *No.* This could be an indication of *burnout*. Meaning, burnout leads to excessive stress that causes emotional exhaustion and exhaustion of the body and mind resulting in a feeling of being overwhelmed and powerless.

You may not be recognizing the person that is hurting you is looking for a reaction from you. Don't engage especially if the person still has anger within his/herself. You are allowed to ignore people without feeling bad. It's your choice. You have the power over your mind and soul.

It is vital that you regain your personal power and not allow other people's misery in your space. The simplest way to do this is by removing them from your surroundings. Or better yet – your life.

I know, it is a lot easier said than done. However, I never said it was going to be easy. Sometimes, the simplest things can be the most difficult things as well. This is why it is important to understand *why* you're doing it to encourage yourself.

Creating boundaries by removing bad energy opens the doors for Positive Vibe Only.

What is Positive Energy?

Positive energy is what keeps us going. Positive energy is a bundle of desirable qualities. A person with enthusiasm, empathy, cheerfulness, optimism, politeness, generosity, and kindness would be ideal. The more positive vibes we create, the deeper state of inner peace we feel, resulting in a sense of well-being, contentment, and productivity.

Identify something you appreciate about someone and tell them that you admire that quality in them. Chances are that this simple comment will resonate with them and make them feel happy – even if for a little while. People feel that positive energy comes from within rather than from outside when you reflect positive vibes back to them based on their own words.

What is Negative Energy?

Negative energy or bad energy is not something measurable enough to be assigned a proper definition. However, we all have encountered negativity at some point in our lives, whether it was within ourselves or from others.

Negative energy often manifests itself as nasty comments – either to your face or behind your back. It is possible to avoid attempting something ambitious if you are aware of your limitations. In some way or another, it brings you down. There is negative energy that comes when you are with certain people. You may not be able to put the finger on it, but this feeling is typically depressing and puts you in a bad mood. Do not let people who are disrespectful and negative influence you. Instead, actively work to eliminate them from your circle.

Question: *Do you feel obligated to allow negativity because it may be a close friend or even a family member?*

Here's the thing: *You're not.*

Set Boundaries to control your well-being!

We feel obligated to allow the negativity because we are afraid to say no or set boundaries. There is no reason to allow these negative people to control your health and well-being. Don't get me wrong; I too am guilty of this.

Over time, I have allowed myself to be emotionally drained by people despite knowing that whenever I encounter them, I am always left feeling drained and exhausted. A negative encounter has either frustrated, angered, or hurt me in a way that I just want to be to myself - just want peace of mind or better yet alone time to think, relax and unwind.

Now, I am making an active effort to regain control over how I choose to spend my time. Based on my personal experience dealing with negative people, this is only my perception. I've learned not to allow anyone to take my peace of mind – to not let other people's behavior destroy your inner peace.

It can be really empowering to understand that you have control over who you want to allow in your life. You do NOT owe anyone your time. Period!

Each one of us knows someone in our lives who is hurtful, frustrating, offensive, and manipulative. Despite the best attempts of surrounding yourself with positive kind people, there will always be some who will disrespect you, insult you, berate you, and misuse you. It is best for you to take control of your life by protecting yourself from the negative effects of this type of behavior by setting clear and firm boundaries with the people in your life.

Question: When was the last time you scheduled something that YOU wanted to do for yourself? Have you ever skipped trying a new restaurant just because you didn't like the way it looked? Do you ever skip a movie you're interested in and instead go for the one all your friends are going to see? If you continue this type of behavior, you may miss out on some extremely fulfilling experiences in your life which can then lead to a lack of interest.

Instead, learn to be your own best friend. Schedule a date with yourself and do something that feeds your mind and spirit away from all the negativity. Enjoy your own company and just let yourself be. It will help you feel present, peaceful, and empowered by your own actions. Go watch a movie by yourself. Go read a book in a coffee shop by yourself. Try something different even if none of your friends want to. Trust me, it will help you so much to venture out of your comfort zone. I am a true testimony to this process!

There are some people who lack positive thinking and are incapable of imagining positive changes in their lives. If you mention a positive change in your life, be prepared to have it shot down immediately by someone who brings negative attention. Seeing the positives in life is your way of embracing change. Any negative person will find an excuse to change your mind if you tell them about this positive mindset. They may even actively discourage you instead of encouraging you. So be prepared for it and don't let them get to your head. Instead, be your own cheerleader and motivate yourself through the good and bad days.

Those who are negative aren't concerned about the amount of energy they drain out of you. It's just a matter of getting their point across. Since they are stuck in their negative state, they aren't concerned about hurting other people's feelings. As a result, they don't listen to others and are not capable of having an open mind. You shouldn't be surprised if they make erratic comments or make accusations against you – especially if you are doing well with your life. They need to spread their negativity to feel validated.

Unfortunately, people with a positive mindset are a good target for these people. It is common for negative people to blame other people for their mistakes. They do not accept full responsibility for their words. Instead, they start blaming others. Their goal is to cast blame on someone else other than themselves. Don't fall for it. Keep distance from those negative people and don't allow them to put you in the position of spreading their negative energy on you. You have things to accomplish – unnecessary distractions are not worth your time or attention.

Negative people fail to see their own negative energy. So don't expect apologies from them right away. When people who have a positive outlook make a mistake, they apologize quickly. This is because they can see both sides of the problem. This is why positive people avoid a negative environment. And to maintain a positive environment, it is necessary to make amends in case someone gets hurt. In every situation, positive people look for the good. Those with negative attitudes secretly hope that positive people fail. Someone close to you, a family member, or even a friend can find themselves caught up in this situation.

People who are positive, encouraging, and supportive want to see others succeed. Don't expect that from a negative person because they don't like to see people grow in a positive manner. They would rather surround themselves with people who have the same energy as them. They will thrive on the "I told you so" if you do fail. However, positive people don't look at failure as a horrible thing, they look at it as a steppingstone to something greater.

Personality-wise, I have reached my breaking point with negative people in my life. As a result, I approach future situations as follows:

Don't Engage:

I know what you're thinking: It's easier said than done. It is important to understand that a positive mindset is more important than the negative people in your life. To do so, you must change your thinking. Make the profound decision that you would not allow any negative energy into your life. Change those negative relationships into acquaintance-ships so that you don't engage them on a deeper level. If it is a family member or a close friend, keep it civil and limit your surroundings and what you say in their presence.

Set Boundaries:

As discussed earlier, YOU have the power to decide who comes into your life and who stays. The moment you notice someone is beginning to drain your energy during an interaction, stop them immediately and say, "sorry to interrupt you but I am not going to entertain or engage in this conversation any longer…excuse me". By stating that you wish to exit this conversation, you are now gaining control of the conversation with an exit plan that is non offensive or hurtful. If they ask why, you can choose to be honest with them and make them aware that you won't allow their negative behavior to affect you. In getting your boundaries in place, you show that you are taking charge of the situation and gaining control of your set boundaries.

Take Care of Yourself:

Negative people can bring the worst out of you. They can trigger you and make you act in ways that you'll likely regret afterwards. Remember that misery loves company, so they thrive on your reaction to their negativity. Consider your well-being and ask yourself, "*Is this really something or someone I wish to put my health at risk over?*" Seek out positive people to keep you balanced.

Consider doing one or more of the following to sustain yourself:
- Surrounding yourself with positive people who love life as much as you do. It could be your family, friend, mentor, coworker or even your pet animals. Your loved ones love you no matter how you are feeling.
- Taking a walk can help you reflect on how blessed you are and what positive things you have in your life.
- Make time to pray and develop a connection with God.
- Take time to read positive quotes and apply them to your daily life.

We all live in a world where negativity permeates every aspect of our lives. There is, however, an option to choose your own life path. Whether you focus on being the negative person who makes people set boundaries is entirely up to you. Alternatively, you can choose to be that person who gives support and encouragement to your people.

The most important thing to remember is to never feel guilty for removing or setting boundaries for people who bring negativity into your life. You are making the right choice for yourself and your well-being. Your life has a purpose, and trust me, it's not to create havoc and spread negativity.

Take control over your circle of friends and protect your heart, mind, soul, and well-being. Pray that these negative people will one day choose positivity over negativity. This decision will have an impact on your health and happiness.

Remove Negative Energy by Eliminating You?

Never give up your power

In situations where there is a lot of negative energy around, you may easily allow that person to steal your joy, or otherwise impact your own state of mind negatively. Don't let the person who has a negative attitude own you; hold onto yourself and your power.

Keep a positive attitude

Think positively. Try to remain optimistic. Show gratitude. Don't let another person's problem define you or your day. Look for the good in your life and don't let other people's negative attitudes get in the way. You have sole responsibility for your life, not anyone else's. Imagine yourself as an individual and remind yourself of that.

Don't pay attention to the perpetrator

If you are entering a situation with a person with negative energy, decide beforehand to ignore them. It becomes easy once you make this decision. You have already chosen to ignore a person, so it is crucial you remind yourself whenever you start thinking you can engage them.

Silence is golden

Essentially, this is similar to ignoring, but a little more active. The silent treatment is normally considered rude when you ignore someone who is talking to you. Studies have shown that, when dealing with difficult people, giving someone the silent treatment may be a better option than communicating with them. This will help you remain calm, cool, and collective in nurturing your own mindset.

Change your space – distance yourself

Sometimes, I find it helpful to remove myself as much as possible from someone else's field to keep myself from absorbing their energy. You can escape their atmosphere if you are having trouble remaining objective and detached from that person. If you tend to be empathetic, you might absorb other people's emotions rather easily. It is important that you recognize this and take any measures necessary to protect yourself.

Take a step back from the person

By pretending they're not there, you can protect yourself from negative people and stay in your own space. Avoiding looking at the person makes this easier to step back and reflect. Look away from that person if you find yourself noticing them too much. This process will get easier as time goes on.

Imagine yourself in a visual way

As you visualize yourself and the energy emanating from you, imagine an atmosphere of positive energy surrounding you. Picture in your mind how it might feel to be surrounded by someone who tends to drain the positivity right out of you. As a method of practice, this is what makes imagery work. Practicing in your mind how you want to see yourself can change the way your mind thinks, similar to the principle of practice makes perfect.

Redirect that negative energy back to the sender

In the event that you still absorb the negativity despite your best efforts, use imagery to visualize yourself removing the negativity from yourself and sending it back to the person who initiated it. During this process, you should stop and think of all the negative emotions you're experiencing. Picture your negativity flowing out of and away from you once you have established this imagery. Lesson learned: don't allow the sender to bring negative energy into your life again.

It's your life... You're responsible for it

As soon as you come to that realization, you realize that you have choices and personal control regarding how others impact you. You have to make sure that you take care of yourself when you are around certain people, whether you like their vibe or not. Their behavior may trigger you. It is your responsibility to manage your emotions, regardless of whether or not they are intentionally antagonizing you.

Positive Energy: How to Get Rid of Negative Energy

One of the biggest enemies that robs you of your potential to become something great is the negative energy that surrounds you. It has a tangible effect on our health, too. Research has shown that people who cultivate negative energy experience more stress, more sickness, and less opportunity over the course of their lives than those who choose to live positively.

Learning how to get rid of negative energy can have a significant effect on your mental health and physical health.

Making a decision to change ourselves into positive people is the first step in finding positive situations and people. Whenever there is a positive experience, the negative energy is pushed away.

Even though both negative and positive energy will always be present, the key to becoming more positive is to fill ourselves up with more positivity in order to reduce the amount of negativity we experience.

This is a lesson to learn for everyone who have encountered a situation from negative people whereas staying positive can help you avoid those angry/hateful/dramatic/toxic mindsets from other people. People will always judge the way you look, think, act, speak or event behave but you must understand that those people see something in you that they admire, or you wouldn't even be the main topic of their conversation.

You will sometimes see a person's negative energy may not even be their own...their carrying someone else's baggage on top of their own baggage. *Not a good thing to deal with...* keep focused on the positivity, don't dwell over someone else's negativity or situation. This will set you back from achieving success in your life. And you will sit back and realize that this was too much baggage for you to even deal with or better yet handle.

What you can do to become more positive and Eliminate Negative Energy

1. Being Grateful for What You Have

When everything in life revolves around us, it's easy to feel that we deserve what we have. Therefore, we identify ourselves as the center of the universe and use this conceit to bring others into our service. If your life is filled with negative thoughts and feelings, you're setting yourself up for a life of unfulfillment.

Positive relationships begin to form when others begin to appreciate our efforts. By opening ourselves to the idea of receiving, we begin to receive more of the things we are grateful for. Taking this step will enrich your life and make it more positive.

2. Laugh More, Especially at Yourself

Sometimes life gets busy, our schedules become full, we get involved in relationships, and work becomes routine-driven and task-oriented. It can be difficult to be human at times. The downside is that this work-driven, serious attitude often creates a negative performance-focused mindset. To avoid getting stuck in this mindset, it is important to not take life too seriously and give yourself a break. You only get one life to live, so why not live it to the fullest?

However, it is important to not take yourself so seriously that you're no longer fun to be around. Learning to laugh at ourselves and our mistakes can help us to live a more authentic life. Finding happiness is a good step towards finding positivity. It is all about finding the balance between seriousness and excitement at the same time.

3. Be Helpful to Others

Negativity and selfishness go hand in hand. People who have a self-centered attitude and do not care about others are only concerned about themselves. When you only have one purpose in life: *take care of yourself and not anyone else,* long-term fulfillment and purpose may not likely be achieved. Look outside yourself and start helping others to get rid of negative energy. Don't ever bite the hand that feeds you.

4. Avoid Negative Energy In Your Thoughts

Either we can be ourselves or we can be our worst enemies. Change begins within. If you want to become more positive, you must change your thought process. Our self-criticism and constant stream of negative self-talk is detrimental to our well-being since we are the hardest on ourselves.

The next time you have a negative thought, try rephrasing it to make it positive. Instead of thinking, *"I can't believe I did so poorly on the exam!"* Try, *"I didn't do as well as I hoped on the exam, but I know next time I will do better. I will study harder for the next one."*

Learning how to change our own self-talk is a very powerful tool. Try to spend a few minutes meditating each day to absorb negative energy if this is particularly challenging for you. Meditation gives your mind a way to recognize negative energy and allow it to be examined and accepted. By learning to identify negative thoughts, you will be able to counter them with your own true words and definition.

5. Build your Success Circle with Positive People

Surrounding yourself with positive, energetic people eliminates the space for negative people. Would you like to know someone who made you feel special, gave you more confidence, or even empowered you? Someone like this will be a positive influence in your life.

Surrounding yourself with like-minded people is what makes you like them. When we associate with negative people and drama queens, we are apt to copy their behavior. When you're surrounded by people that don't show positive behavior, it's difficult to improve.

Make it your priority to limit your exposure to negative influences. Spend time with positive people instead. Make sure you surround yourself with positive, successful go-getters who are supportive and caring of you. Don't forget to nurture and protect your relationships with those who bring you positive energy.

By bringing your own positive energy to your circle, you will be able to create an atmosphere of positivity within it. Always seek out honest and open people who will tell you the truth without hurting your feelings. Those whom you know will either start liking the new you or become resistant to your positive change as your attitude grows.

Making changes in your life is intimidating but letting go of the negative people in your life has a fantastic impact on your overall well-being. It is also an important step in finding positive relationships. People with positive perspectives bounce views off each other. When you think positively on your own, the process is slow, but when you are surrounded by positive people, the experience becomes exponential.

6. Transform Negative Energies into Positive Actions

I find it difficult to navigate negative thoughts and energy. In order to remove negative energy, you need to turn it into positive actions. Next time you're in one of these situations and feeling bad, take a break and walk away. Close your eyes and take a deep breath.

As soon as you are calm, write down your thoughts on paper while you analyze the situation. Identify four or five actions or solutions to begin solving the problem. You will solve more problems rationally and be happier if you move away from the emotionally charged negative energies and move in the direction of action-oriented positives.

While you may not be able to solve all your problems with just a few minutes, taking a break is still beneficial to your effectiveness. The feeling of clearing your mind will aid you in being more able to think clearly to solve whatever problem you're facing.

7. Take Full Responsibility of Your Own Actions

You are responsible for your own actions. Making excuses and blaming others only impedes your efforts to change negative energies. One of the most important steps in creating a more positive life is taking full responsibility for your life, your thoughts, and your actions.

You have the power to change your life, change your thoughts, and create your own reality. If we internalize this idea deeply, you can realize that no one is able to control you or your actions. It is up to you to determine how you relate to people and circumstances. Taking positive steps towards yourself will help you take full responsibility of your own actions in life.

Setting Boundaries from the Outside

When you allow someone to influence you negatively, you are receiving negative energy from the outside. Is that something you are willing to allow? For example: not creating healthy boundaries for people.

There are many people who find it difficult to establish healthy boundaries; some people need to please others and can only do so when they are angry. You may experience pain as an empath through the pain of others. You may lack self-esteem and feel as if whatever you do was never enough. You may also feel guilty if you don't help them.

In the beginning, you may not be aware of the effects, however you will feel them almost immediately; including sudden pain, inability to concentrate, confusion, discomfort, restlessness, nausea, and mood swings.

The Perception of Negative Energy

Negative energy in a person can be seen by paying attention to their actions and recognizing their symptoms. These include:

- Tendency to quickly absorb other people's negativity
- Anxiety and restlessness
- Sleepless
- Having trouble controlling your thoughts and feelings
- Fear and anxiety
- Headaches
- Tiredness and exhaustion
- Depression
- Suicidal ideation
- Dependency on drugs or alcohol
- Inability to control one's behavior
- Prefer to be in dark places
- Hoarding and dirty surroundings

Don't let negative people hold you back. Forgive your past.

Holding onto repetitive thoughts about the things that have hurt you in the past not only causes you to relive that pain, but also invites negative energy back into your life.

You are in a vulnerable position. Forgiving does not mean letting someone off the hook for what they have done to you, but it does mean protecting yourself moving forward. In truth, letting go of the pain and the energy you are holding onto because of reliving an event, is all that needs to be done.

The presence of negative people in your life is not something anyone likes, wants, or asks for.

There is only one thing holding you back from forgiveness is "fear". You are afraid you are going to be hurt again, you are afraid you will have to change, you are afraid your peers will perceive you as weak, and you are afraid you will become too soft.

You cannot live a loving, open life if you are fearful. If you are working on forgiveness and opening your heart, you may experience painful feelings and memories. Keeping an open mind and forgiving others far outweighs the downsides.

Being open and removing all the blocks that are holding you back allows yourself to experience a level of maturity. When you carry anger, you end up hurting yourself more and more every time that situation or person occurs back into your life. Why would you want to continue hurting yourself? You'll never move forward unless you let go.

However, it is important to understand that forgiving doesn't mean that you must allow the person back into your life. The relationship equation you have with them depends on their importance in your life, the intensity of their mistake, as well as their willingness to rectify their behavior.

If it's someone important to you and they are genuinely working hard to change the behavior that caused them to hurt you, then it would be acceptable to give them another chance. Even then, it is necessary that you do. You can forgive them while also cutting ties with them.

89

On the other hand, if the person isn't willing to change their behavior, then it would make no sense to allow them any space in your life. In such cases, it is important to forgive them in order to let go of the anger and resentment in your heart – whether or not they ask for forgiveness. At the same time, it is equally important to NOT let them back into your life.

People believe that forgiving someone's means that you have to go back to how things were before the mistake was made. However, that's far from being the reality. You can forgive someone, while also acknowledging that you don't want them in your life anymore.

Self-love comes from forgiving others. *What does self-love mean?* We all have different ways of taking care of ourselves, so self-love can mean something different for each of us.

Self-love is an important part of mental health. Finding out what that looks like for you is important. Self-love is a state of self-acceptance that is fostered by actions that promote our physical, psychological, and spiritual health. You cannot love yourself fully unless you value your own happiness and well-being. Being self-loving means taking care of your own needs and not sacrificing your well-being for others.

I Will Not Allow Negativity to Take Over My Life: Step-by-Step Process

Step 1: Decide That You Are Worth It

Whenever you get tired of being tired with a certain person, it usually indicates that you're at the end of your rope. If you want to achieve your goals and become the person you want to be, you must believe that you are worthy of it.

Now is the time to dedicate yourself to yourself, your dreams, and your goals. Think about the negative outcomes from holding onto these people in your life, as well as the impact of their influence on your goals and happiness.

Step 2: Identify The Toxic People

Avoid toxic relationships. My advice has always been to eliminate toxicity from your life. Toxic relationships often come hand-in-hand with negativity. If someone makes you feel bad about who you are, how you live, or what you do, then that person is toxic.

Toxic people feel better about themselves when they tend to hurt others to make themselves feel better. Let them cultivate a better relationship with themselves because in the long run, they will need it. Keep an eye out for people who negatively influence your other relationships, invade your space, and take up a lot of your time. When someone makes you feel uncomfortable or unproductive, that's a red flag.

The problem with toxic people is they are victimized (or being victimized) and tend to bring down your energy level and keep the focus on them and their problems the whole time. Having someone share with you their struggles/challenges is different from having someone always complain about their own.

Step 3: Let Them Go By Establishing Boundaries

You must set boundaries in order to keep your sanity, well-being, and happiness. People who do not respect your boundaries don't respect you. You need to elicit your own personal boundary list, and not be afraid to speak up when others cross it. Regardless of the method you choose, be sure to stay firm in delivering what you need to be satisfied.

Step 4: Remind Yourself Daily Why & Don't Feel Guilty

Some may find this silly, but the power of belief can be a huge asset in life. The decisions you make in your life are ultimately up to you. You should remind yourself of it every day. Although it reflects your natural pattern, you are not abandoning these people in fact you are allowing them to discover their own path and place in life while maintaining your own.

Step 5: Bring In The Positive

You get to decide how you want your life to look and it starts with who you choose to surround yourself with. Find people who will support your ambitions, help you to be a better person, encourage your ideas

91

because they know how important it is for *you* and ultimately share your views. Your career will rise to greater heights if you surround yourself with bright and successful people like you.

Here's How to Begin Taking Action Today
Take 5 minutes and think about the people you spend the most time with - at home, in the workplace, at school, practice, etc.

Who are they?
Who are the positive influencers?
Who are the negative influencers?
Now, look at your list of negative influencers and begin to slowly reduce the amount of time you spend in those relationships by following the steps above.

How to Distance Yourself from Negativity:
Negative people should be avoided. This may sound so obvious, but when was the last time you questioned yourself, *"Is this person having a positive or negative impact on me?"* In many instances, we choose whom we interact with. Yet, we somehow tend to fail avoiding the negatives and go with the flow when it comes to who's around us. Keep your eyes open and keep in mind how people make you feel. If you feel a negative vibe towards that person (you'll know if you feel drained, down, or just icky after spending time with the person), limit your interactions.

We've all heard the phrase, *"misery loves company,"* right? And it's true. Learn how to deal with negative people by learning to control yourself. This includes your attention, time, focus, energy, words, and actions. While negative energy can steal your joy and positive energy, it can't succeed unless you allow it to affect you.

Look for positive inspiration. There is a lot of negativity in the world, but there is also a lot of positivity. Discover individuals, activities, support groups, educational websites, etc. that will inspire you to do better. When you are having a down day, having some resources that you can reach out to when you're feeling negative can really make a difference. Look for positive mentors who will help you reach your full potential, call a friend to lift your spirit or a close family member. This will most likely do the trick.

What Boundaries Will You Set For Yourself – Activity?

Take a moment to envision what it will be like once we start setting healthy boundaries for ourselves. Think of a person or group which you have difficulties setting healthy boundaries with.

What are some specific measures you should take to strengthen your boundaries?
Are you concerned about the reaction of other's pertaining to these changes?
When you set healthy boundaries, how do you expect your life to change?

Which of the following are your boundaries, if any, with the person you listed above?

Each boundary category should have a check-mark in the appropriate column below.

Rigid Boundaries

A person who is constantly keeping others at a distance (emotionally, physically, or otherwise) is considered to have rigid boundaries.

Avoids close relationships.
Not likely to ask for help.
Is not close to many people.
Information is highly protected.
To avoid possible rejection, keeps other people at a distance.

Porous Boundaries

A person who tends to get too involved with others have porous boundaries. People with high levels of dependence on other people often experience feelings of anxiety, burnout, and desire to please others.

Have difficulty saying no to others' requests.
Oversharing personal information.
Saying "no" to requests from others is difficult.
Overly involved in others' problems.
The opinion of others can influence a decision.

Used to being disrespected.

They fear rejection if they fail to comply with others.

Healthy Boundaries

A person who values their own opinion has healthy boundaries.

Doesn't compromise values for other people.

Sharing personal information in an appropriate manner (not oversharing or under-sharing).

Has an understanding of the wants and needs of others and is able to communicate them?

Being able to accept "no" from others.

Boundary Categories	Porous	Rigid	Healthy
Physical Boundaries			
Mental Boundaries			
Emotional Boundaries			
Time Boundaries			

Imagining establishing healthy boundaries with this person is a great way to get a sense of what it'll be like. Your boundaries might need to be loosened if they are too rigid. They must set limits and say "no" if they are porous.

Healthy Boundaries Questions

1. Explain what "healthy boundaries" are and why they are important to you.
2. Identify your personal limits by using the following strategies:
    a) Identifying Your Limits: Clarifying your emotional, psychological, physical, and spiritual limits. Be aware of what you are capable of tolerating and accepting, as well as what makes you uncomfortable and stressed.
    b) Be Attentive To Your Feelings: Pay attention to the three key feelings that are often cues that you need to establish boundaries:
        - Discomfort
        - Resentment
        - Guilt

If you're experiencing uncomfortable feelings, resentment, or guilt in a particular situation, person, or area of your life, you should set or adjust boundaries accordingly.

    c) Remind Yourself That You Are Entitled To Set Boundaries: When you fear what someone else will think if you set or enforce boundaries, remind yourself that this right indeed belongs to you.

    d) Think About Your Environment: Your environment can either assist you in setting boundaries or hinder your efforts.

"Everything negative – pressure, challenges – is all an opportunity for me to rise."

~Kobe Bryant

Chapter 8
Elements of Dimensions in Life: Who?
Your Support System

Family is everything to me – My family is my foundation of true happiness and success in life. My family keeps me grounded, safe, and humbled, and provides me with unconditional love which is truly a blessing.

~Dr. Christina S. Rogers

Successful Relationships

A support system can consist of family members, friends, colleagues, classmates, mentors, or someone who is important in your life. In order for a relationship to succeed, both parties must contribute. The golden rule is to treat your friends as you would like to be treated. Basically, be the friend you want to have.

Show Your Appreciation

Your family and friends are important to you - thank them for what they do for you. Showing appreciation can go a long way

Must Stay In Touch

Whether it be through phone calls, text messages, emails, or any other form of communication. Remember to keep in touch and check-in on your loved ones often. It's important to stay in touch as much as possible. It could damage the relationship as time goes by with limiting your interaction.

Make Yourself Available When Needed

True friends stick with you when the going gets tough. Give your friends a safe place to confide in you. You should give them free rein to express themselves without judgement. However, always protect your own well-being and sanity during the conversation.

Some people prefer to always be the one who offers support instead of accepting it. The self-image of being 'strong' and 'together' might be the reason why some fear becoming dependent.

However, friends and family members often want to feel they have done something good for you. Allow them! Accepting help can be of great benefit to you. You also acknowledge that you value the contributions your friends and loved ones make, which helps keep the relationship balanced.

Support the Success in Others

Whenever someone you care about succeeds, you will be thrilled. You can acknowledge to yourself that you are a little jealous, but don't let your bond be broken. That jealousy bone should get you motivated even more to accomplish your goals to succeed much higher.

Research suggests that healthy and supportive families share the following qualities:

Share Appreciation:
Make sure your family members know how much you care about them. How much you appreciate them for going above and beyond. An example of something simple might be saying thanks for making you laugh or spending time with you. Make sure you're sincere. Family relationships can be strengthened by always expressing appreciation.

Quality Family Time Together:
It's great to have time to spend with family at mealtimes, play games together, and do things together as a family. You can spend time with your family in countless ways to strengthen your bond. For example, my family and I have a "group message" where we communicate through text often to share family updates, events, accomplishments, play games and even tell jokes to one another…just having fun creating special memories that will last forever.

However, you must make sure that family time is quality time, not quantity time. Whenever you are with a loved one, you should make sure you give them all of your attention. Turn off your phone and be present in the moment.

Healthy Communication:

Families can find it hard to communicate, especially when there are so many places to be and things to do throughout the day. Having supportive families improves the quality of communication and emotional safety within the family.

It's important to communicate your love and support for one another. The more you express your unwavering support, the more comfortable they will be talking to you about their problems, concerns, and triumphs.

Individual Accountability:

Families need to hold each other accountable for what they promise and promise not to do. When someone fails to come through, you are unable to build a strong family which is a big part of how strong a family is. Support is also important when a family member is struggling. By helping them through the tough times, you will bring your family closer together. – Family is everything!

Life Dimensions: People's Dimensions Change Overtime

These dimensions are my safe zone; my support system that I created for myself. Support can come from family, friends, pets, neighbors, or someone/something you feel that will benefit you towards your success in life. Support comes in many shapes and forms. It is helpful to have a variety of different resources to lean on.

Take a moment to think about your life dimensions – your value support system. To give you a glimpse of my world, I have listed my life dimensions on my value support system table chart below. List yours?

Value Support System	
GOD_____	Business/Job
Family_____	Church
Friends_____	Self-Care/Meditation
Pets_____	Music & Dance
Education_____	Technology

Your Family Support System

In a healthy family system, you are surrounded by individuals who have a positive relationship with you, who are supportive of your choices and trials, and who are there through both the good and bad times in life - they don't give up when the going gets tough. It is one of the most valuable things your family can possess.

Creating a strong, supportive family system can be a tireless and challenging endeavor, but it is well worth it. Others may have friends, coworkers, or even just one or two trusted individuals as part of their family support system. A strong family is one of the most valuable treasures you can have to ensure your family thrives.

Building Your Support System

Whether you are building a family support system or strengthening the one that you already have, you must do what benefits you the most. As one of the sayings goes, *"we teach people how to treat us."* The same is true when looking for a family support system. You can show your love and trust by supporting those you love and trust most.

Keep encouraging them to succeed in their healthy goals and to overcome life's challenges. Become the support system you are seeking for from your own family. Think about those people you trust and love in your life and consider ways you can deepen your connection with them. Based on your interactions, you'll be able to judge if they're willing to have a deeper, authentic, and transparent relationship. Can you count on them for encouragement and for showing interest in your life?

Describe how they have had a positive impact on your life and how you would love to have them join your support system. Your loved ones and trusted family members should know how they can support you. If you are surrounded by people who positively influence and care for you, your family is more likely to succeed!

Family Support is the Most Important Factor of Success
Why Are Families Important to Individuals?

A variety of factors contribute to the importance of family support for individuals like myself, the majority of which are connected to personal well-being. There is nothing like family to provide you with physical, emotional, and mental health benefits like none other.

Families are the first places where people learn how to live life, observe, love one another, communicate, cook, clean, and support each other's goals and aspirations. Families are often considered to be the smallest social group, and they also teach you about the most important foundations of life. As an example, they teach you the norm and value of life and what is right and wrong.

My family still gives me love and affection, plus inspiration for me to excel in my life plans which plays a huge role in helping me achieve my goals and especially helping others. With family support, people may develop successful characteristics that will guide them on their journey to success. Families therefore serve as the first learning environment in their lives, as well as a social and economic support system.

When you look back, you will realize that you relied on a variety of people in different stages of your life. Our support system has different members in it that we turn to for help in different areas of our lives, depending on our age, needs, wants, and desires. As important as it is to receive support, it is equally important to give support.

The Benefits of a Strong Support System

Sense of Belonging: We all need to feel a sense of belonging throughout our lives. In order to develop a sense of self we learn from our family and friends as we transition from childhood to adulthood. The right support system can allow you to reach your full potential, no matter what area you are striving for.

Stress Relief: Stress is reduced when you have a solid support system. It can be therapeutic to spend time with your loved ones and reduce anxiety. If you need help reducing stress, consider taking a walk, a hike, or a yoga class with a friend. An effective support system can help you relax after a stressful day.

Improve Self-Esteem: A person can feel better about themselves when they have someone they can depend on for support and who can depend on them for support. It is always good to feel as though others are rooting for you on the sidelines, as well as those who are part of your support system. Many of us in the world have found ourselves in new cities or locations where we do not know anyone. The idea is to connect with people with similar interests as you by volunteering, taking a course, learning music, or joining a book club that can gradually build your support group.

Reasons Why Family Is Important:

Family is something everyone is born into, but not everyone gets the chance to cultivate a strong one. It is common for those who lack a good birth family to build a new family later in life. What does family mean to you? How does it affect a person as a child and as an adult? Does it really matter at all?

Connections Begin In The Family:

Having a relationship with one's parents (guardian) and siblings is the first relationship a child will have. Healthy or unhealthy, these relationships provide a model for how future relationships will be like. Choosing friends and partners based on how similar they are to your family is often unintentional, but you could say that people often consider the degree to which their behavior is similar to yours. It reinforces beliefs about relationships and about oneself as a result of repeated dynamics in the family.

Family Is Essential During Challenging Times:

People need support when life gets tough. As well as financial support, this includes emotional support as well. It is a family's role to provide encouragement and love during difficult times if someone relies on them. When going through a personal crisis, feeling accepted and understood is a basic need.

Families Are A Source Of Affection And Encouragement:

Families provide a sense of belonging. People seeking happiness can benefit from the affection and encouragement their families provide, in either good or bad times. People with strong families are able to receive the love and support they need in all situations. Motivated by their family, an individuals will find the courage and motivation to succeed. However, if a person does not receive love and support from a family structure, they will feel hopeless, depressed, and even lonely.

101

People Raised In Close-Knit Families Have Closer Connections Throughout Their Lifetimes:

Families teach values. Research indicates that people from close-knit families go on to enjoy close connections throughout their lives. A person's family structure teaches them more than merely life lessons. It teaches them a value system. It is a matter of learning what is right and wrong for their family, as well as what is important to their community. As a person grows up, these values become part of their identity. Values influence how a person treat others, how they view themselves, and what they see as their purpose in life. Your close-knit family are the people who will and should push you to reach higher towards your success. Let that resonate with you for a minute.

Activity Lesson for YOU

Now take a moment to think about your life and who are important to you as it relates to your value support system. *Table chart, page 98.*

Look at my value support system table chart to get a better idea of the activity lesson. Design your own table chart of values you desire. Be creative. Place your table chart somewhere easily accessible – like placing it on the wall, refrigerator, your bedroom, or your work desk, etc… – and look at your table chart everyday to remind yourself what's important to you in your life. This activity lesson will help you to appreciate your value support system even more.

"I learned a lot in my life by paying attention and listening to how people around me worked."

~Kris Jenner

The knowledge that FAMILY is important allows me to express my gratitude for my family more fully and help others better understand and appreciate the value of their family support system. By being goal-oriented and committed to achieving excellence, I was able to achieve success with the support of my family.

During the good times and the bad times, they have always challenged me, loved me to the core, and supported me to the end. I've learned as generations pass, families become stronger, cherished, supported, and strengthens one another which makes the bond grow even stronger.

As we go through life, we gradually forget what makes us unique and what makes us different from others, but we never forget that family makes us who we are today and leaves an imprint that lives on forever. Thank you, family!

Chapter 9
Networking through Mentor-ship: Establishing Connections to Build Relationships

Networking has the purpose of forming mutually beneficial relationships. It is important to approach business and personal relationships authentically in order to achieve success because people do not like to feel that they are being used or "sold to." Instead, they prefer building a relationship that helps them reach their goals or improve their lives.

Here's how to cultivate genuine, mutually beneficial relationships.

Be True To Yourself

In order to form a genuine and lasting connection, it is important to consistently be yourself. Make it clear what you value to others. You will inspire others with your passion. Consider what you can do for others rather than just focusing on what they can do for you. Your relationship will evolve into a trust-based one if you respond in a kind manner.

Be Honest About Your Intentions

When it comes to building these relationships with authenticity, you simply can't force it. Make sure to be sincere about your intentions and don't begin a conversation just to gain something from the other person. You might even consider offering them a favor before expecting a return. If you start building relationships this way, it will lead to long-term relationships that are authentic and genuine.

The Key To Success Is Relationships—Fostering Genuine Connections In Your Career:

Based on my efforts, my career success has been driven by the relationships I have built. I made concerted efforts to create genuine connections with those around me in every role I took on. I worked hard not only on the tasks I was assigned but, on the people, as well. As a team player, I seek to gain the trust and respect of my colleagues, and especially the leadership team who changed my career path.

Relationships are everything, both personally and professionally. The people in my life who have been supportive of me played a major role in my success. My desire to learn and accomplish more pushed me to take a chance and apply the knowledge I have learned from others to myself.

Your career will be defined by these types of relationships. Here are some ways to cultivate them:

Keep Your Commitments - What You Say Is What You Do!

When you say you'll do something, follow through with it no matter what. If, for any reason, you are struggling to do so, make it known in advance and apologize for it. Any relationship, strong or weak, will crumble if you don't follow through on commitments.

Think about how you can help the other person and what you can bring to the relationship. You must fulfill your promise. Reliable relationships are based on proving trustworthiness.

Know You Won't Click With Everyone, And That's Okay

Some people you will love and want to get to know, and some you will dismiss. You don't need to fake a relationship with someone just because you feel like you have to.

The most important thing to remember is that to create a genuine relationship, you need to be hungry to learn more, to improve at what you do, and to benefit from the insights of other people who know their industries.

Genuine, mutually beneficial connections can be the key to learning new skills quickly, getting a backdoor reference, and leveraging connections in unexpected career-changing ways.

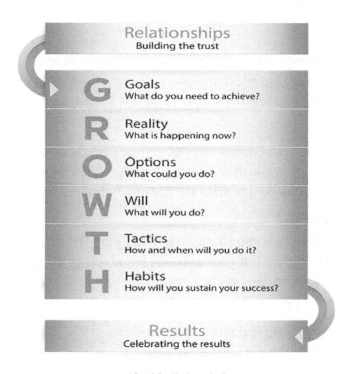

You can build meaningful relationships in the following ways:

Discuss the Things That Matter to You

When two individuals realize they share similar interests and values, they establish the strongest of relationships. These points of commonality regarding interests and values are what create the strongest emotional connection.

Give others a chance to know what matters to you and what you believe in by sharing your beliefs and caring. The same things matter to them, so they will tell you if they believe in the same things. The result will be that your shared knowledge will give you a sense of belonging.

Be honest with the people around you, even when this will initially hurt them. It's more important for them to trust you than not to feel hurt. And always do what you promised. Even better, think twice before you promise anything, and only promise what you really can and are willing to do.

Strengthening relationships requires support as well. A solid relationship between people depends on their ability to rely on each other in times of need, whether that support is a few kind words or a series of massive actions.

As a result, you cannot meet everyone's needs constantly. You have limited resources, such as time and energy. However, you can at least try to be there for the people who are genuinely important to you.

The Bottom Line Is:

In your life, you can strengthen many kinds of relationships and advance them to the best of your abilities by adopting the right mindset and behavior. With strong bonds, not only do you feel more fulfilled but also connected to everyone and everything around you.

As a result, you feel more alive, and you enjoy living in the moment. You have the opportunity to explore a whole world of possibilities.

Business Tips For Building Relationships:

Your career success and your sanity depend on establishing meaningful relationships with others. Understanding why we as humans crave and value relationships was crucial to me, and so was learning to build meaningful relationships in my career.

Tell me, *what happens when you don't have the right relationships in your life?*

Based on research and my reflections, the following insight shares the comfort provided by relationships:

- The feeling of being connected (*knowing we aren't alone*)
- Support (*knowing there is help available*)
- Validation (*being aware that others feel the same way*)

I reflected on how many times I had turned to someone with who I had built a relationship with for one of these three reasons (connection, support, or validation).

Many times!

If I hadn't had those relationships, what would have happened?

If I didn't have a connection, support, or validation at the time - and more importantly, right now - where would I be?

There's no doubt about it: *I would not be where I am right now.*

Having all this knowledge together just proves what everyone always says: *networking and building relationships are essential.*

Furthermore, it helped me understand how crucial relationships are at the very base level; by understanding where I would be - or where I wouldn't be - without relationships.

I will now present my challenge: *how do you build relationships with other people?*

There are so many times when people realize the importance of networking and who they know but don't know how to approach approaching those relationships in a way that doesn't feel aggressive or slimy.

Therefore, I wondered... *Are we unsure how to do something or are we just uncomfortable with the idea?*

Maybe we don't feel confident enough?

Perhaps, we are not sure where to begin?

Every individual has a unique personality, so how you build relationships may be different from how I do it. Yet, I believe very strongly in the four steps below that will help you build relationships with people. If nothing else, it will put you on the path to success - regardless of your personality or where you are when it comes to building meaningful relationships.

Starting Out: 4-Step-Process:

Intend To Accomplish Something Specific

Understanding why you want to do something is the first step towards most things in life.

How do you plan to build a particular relationship in business?

Consider these examples:
- Having weekly meetings with a partner who can act as an accountability partner….
- Finding someone who occupies the position I desire so that I can learn from them….
- Engaging in joint ventures or affiliate relationships….

Interested In Learning More:

You aren't the only one interested in what's happening around you; remember, this isn't only about you. Listen to their story, learn about their background, and discover what drives them.

Questions such as:
- What motivated you to get involved in what you're currently working on?
- What is something you are really looking forward to?
- Any questions regarding your type of business or profession?

By asking questions such as these, you'll start a natural conversation that will help you discover more about their interests and what's important to them.

Learn as much as possible about them and offer value whenever you can. Maybe you know someone who can provide an introduction, or maybe you can share your knowledge or expertise to help them.

Keeping Up By Following Up

Relationships don't happen overnight. Taking the initiative, staying engaged, and pursuing them takes time and patience.

Following up on what you discussed at an event or conference will help initiate the relationship by sending the person an email afterward and following up on whatever it was you discussed with them at the event or conference. Ask them what the biggest takeaway was and how they plan to apply that to their own business. Do you have any idea on how you might be able to help? Bringing the conversation over to email would allow you to learn more about each other, including what you have in common with one another.

Be Yourself And Don't Overthink It

Throughout human history, relationships have been central to human existence. Our desire and value for relationships stem from their intrinsic importance to us. So just be yourself! Connecting with others and building meaningful relationships in business isn't something you need to overthink.

What Does a Good Working Relationship Looks Like?
Working relationships are based on trust, respect, open communication, self-awareness, and inclusion. Here are some characteristics to explore.

Your honesty, thoughts and actions are open when you trust your team members. It saves you time and energy because you don't have to "watch your back."
The whole team works towards the goal together. A team that values each other's input values each other's insight, wisdom, and creativity. Think of inclusion not just as accepting diverse viewpoints but also as welcoming them. For instance, when your colleagues have different perspectives from your own, consider their insights and perspectives when making a decision.
Good relationships are based on open and honest communication. The more effectively you communicate with others either by sending an email or an instant message or even meeting in person, or through video cam, the more reliable you are building a connection.

Understanding Your Relationship Needs

How well do you know what others expect from you? And do you know what they need from you? Understanding these needs can be instrumental in building better relationships.

Learn How To Be An Effective People's Person

The first step to building good relationships is to develop good people skills. If you are not good at communicating with people, it can get very difficult to form healthy relationships. However, if you follow the tips outlined in this chapter, you can learn to develop these skills very effectively.

Learn How To Practice Mindful Listening

Those who truly listen to the people they encounter with respond better. Talking less and understanding more will be possible if you practice mindful listening. Then, you'll be known as someone who can be trusted and willing to learn by listening.

Networking Tips You Should Follow:
- Aim high in networking
- Learn where to network
- Know who to reach out to
- Reach out as a first step
- Make networking a priority
- Provide the most value you can
- Introduce people and make an effort to connect with others

What are Networking Skills?

Networking skills include the abilities you need to maintain professional relationships. Many industries rely on networking for sales, business development, and many other functions to complete their task. Bringing new contacts together and promoting something valuable requires networking skills.

111

Mentor-ship can be a great asset for you. The key to a successful mentor relationship is to understand what makes them tick.

Throughout your career, a mentor can offer guidance on everything from difficult decisions to managing your time. You can take your career to the next level if you get feedback from someone more experienced. Both mentors and mentee must devote themselves to making a mentor relationship successful.

What Does a Mentor Do?

Everybody needs a confidant that they can turn to when they need advice. Regardless of what stage you are in in your life, mentors can serve as a valuable resource.

An experienced mentor can help you develop your skills as a leader, a strategist, a consultant, or a manager. In the entrepreneurial sector, a mentor can help your startup through common challenges among startups like funding, paperwork, finding clients, and delivering on projects for instance.

Nevertheless, as with any relationship, maintaining a successful mentoring relationship is hard work but you must be opened to fulfill that need.

Building a Mentor Relationship

Building your relationship with your mentor is like searching for a job – you need to take the time, effort, and focus necessary to grow it, achieve it, and do it.

Four Tips Mentee Can Use To Build A Successful Relationship With their Mentors

Decide What You Want To Accomplish

First, identify your objectives - this will help you decide who will be a good mentor for you. Consider questions such as:

What do you hope to gain from the relationship?

What would you like to give to build the relationship?

Mentors can only be of help once you determine which type of support and guidance you require. Once you determine the type of support and guidance you require, finding the right match becomes crucial.

Become Familiar With Your Mentor

You need to get to know each other before forging any kind of relationship. This is particularly important in a mentoring relationship.

When it comes to relationship building with colleagues and mentors, the same rules apply. Discover the person's professional background and interests.

A mentor is more likely to be able to help you if you know more about them. Ask them how they've overcome educational or career challenges and about their professional backgrounds.

Keep In Touch

Your mentoring relationship needs to be maintained through regular communication. Follow through consistently. Regular check-ins, such as monthly phone calls or face-to-face meetings are some of the best ways to build the best relationships. Keep in touch more often and keep that relationship alive.

Understand What Will Be Expected Of You

Good mentors seek out individuals who take an active role in their careers. They are eager to learn and want to add value where they can. Show your mentor that you're eager to progress in your educational or career journey by being prepared to meet to create an action plan for success.

Be prepared to face your mentor with specific agendas. Provide an outline of what you wish to discuss when you see your mentor. By the end of your meeting, you and your mentor should feel like you've met your objectives.

Two valuable objectives are achieved through this strategy. Each time you meet with your mentor, you are able to learn something specific and useful. Mentors can be prepared to guide you with their best advice when you provide them with this information.

You will also demonstrate to your mentor that you are taking the mentor-ship serious and taking advantage of the time you both have. In addition, the mentor becomes happier about the relationship that they built and the work that they do.

Know When To Let Go

Often, career aspirations and paths change. Relationships with mentors aren't meant to last forever, and that's okay. Although mentor-ship is a valuable resource, it is important to know when the relationship is over. Give yourself time to rethink the situation before ending your relationship.

Give Thanks To Your Mentor

Thank you goes a long way. Your mentor will appreciate your time and advice if you let them know. Your gratitude should be expressed throughout the relationship. A handwritten thank-you note, or email will make that effort worthwhile.

Everyone needs time to do things they love, and a mentor's time is valuable in meeting with you, answering your emails, and helping you advance overall. If you're working with a mentor, tell them how much you appreciate their advice. You can even go out of your way to show a small gesture of gratitude verbally in person as well.

What Is The Best Length Of Time For A Mentoring Relationship?

Mentoring is not a one-size-fits-all relationship. The relationship may last if it is mutually beneficial for both. Relationships between mentors and mentee are often lifelong, they grow more equitable as time passes.

You may have time requirements to follow if you're part of a formal mentor-ship program, so make sure you're aware of them. By knowing the guidelines, you also show that you are a good candidate for mentor-ship and that you are serious about it.

What Are The Benefits Of Mentoring?

When you have a good mentor relationship, you have access to advice, strategy, and a deeper understanding of the world you are working in. An effective mentor relationship can help you define and understand your job role, work through any problems at work and empower you to do your best work which in turn can lead to promotions in corporate settings or long-term business success for entrepreneurs.

The perspective provided by a mentor can help you be your best if you are willing to engage, listen, ask questions, and cultivate the relationship.

When the relationship is built on trust and connection, the mentor-ship is powered by the phrase *'Success with No Stress.'*

Relationships between Mentors and Mentee: Key To Successful Mentor-ship

Mentoring is undoubtedly a valuable experience that is crucial to growth and development. Mentor and mentee relationships need to be constructed in a supportive environment so that both parties can build trust, set goals, and achieve them by identifying creative problem-solving issues and solutions.

While mentor-mentee relationship cannot exist without the other, there's a clear separation between their roles. Let's learn about their roles before developing an effective strategy for this relationship.

What Is The Role Of A Mentor?

The definition of a mentor is someone with expertise, experience, or knowledge that other people can benefit from, and who strongly believes in sharing their knowledge with others. By learning about people's strengths and leveraging them to create solutions, they act as a guide, advisor, and support structure to bring out the best in them.

Mentors recognize the unique challenges and circumstances that each individual faces. One person's advice may not apply to someone else. Using this information helps them to understand their mentee's unique challenges and give advice that is tailored to their needs.

The value of mentoring is that the mentor shares their experiences, learnings, and advice, but also gives the other person space and time to develop their own solutions, and look beyond their own mental blocks, and avoid mistakes they have made in the past. An idea that does not align with their beliefs does not threaten them or cause them to reject it. Instead, they encourage the other person to express themselves by actively listening to the person.

What Is The Role Of A Mentee?

The mentor-mentee relationship sets its tone when the latter takes on the role of mentor. The mentoring relationship is driven by the mentee's determination of the role model they wish to emulate and the goals they need to accomplish.

Over time, the relationship grows as they take actions that build upon each other. Regardless of whether their mentor's advice is acted upon or not, they never hesitate to speak their mind or share their opinion. They are responsible for keeping their mentor informed when they wish to deviate from the original agreement or decide to follow a different path based on their learnings along the way.

Great mentee know the areas of their growth and development and look for a mentor who respects the type of knowledge they possess. When they learn their limits and set boundaries for their learning, they may approach multiple mentors. They strive to learn from each of their mentors.

An excellent mentor asks the following questions frequently:
Why is this person a good mentor for me?
Why should I be helped by my mentor?
Do I understand what my mentor expects from the partnership?
And how can I provide that?
Am I'm open to sharing my ideas?" Am I'm being heard?
Is there anything that I can do to grow this relationship?
Is their feedback taken seriously?

Mentor-mentee relationships are based on mutual respect and personal connection. Building trust and aligning with one another's values are crucial to cultivating a relationship. As relationships grow, they also change. Staying in the old may means continuing in a relationship you don't want to be in or continuing with old ways of doing things when there are new and improved ways to achieve the same goals. People may need to evaluate a relationship for the sake of their future needs, regardless of how it may have fulfilled their needs in the past. Taking into account of the new knowledge can determine what needs to be changed by understanding the four key effective strategies:

Strategy #1: Commit To Each Other

Mentor-ship demands commitment and dedication. To succeed in a mentor-mentee relationship, time is of utmost importance, but it also demands a great deal of energy to engage, guide, and deal with the ups and downs and all the human emotions involved when two people commit to each other.

Commitment to each other and respect for their time are needed to ensure a genuine meeting of the minds. I highly recommend that both mentor and mentee write down their commitments and refer to them periodically.

Mentors may commit to the following as a way to express their commitment:

My commitment to my mentee is both physically and mentally available at our agreed upon time,
It's important that I give honest advice and not withhold information or make any public statements that are not accurate,
Engaging in active listening will allow me to listen to my mentee's ideas without applying my beliefs and opinions as filters,
Taking the responsibility of helping my mentee reach their goals is a major responsibility,
When it comes to sharing my true feelings and thoughts about my mentee, I will be honest and transparent,
I take complete responsibility for my own success during the process,
I will be honest in my feelings and thoughts with my mentor at all times.

Strategy #2: Connect Relationship Through Trust

Mentor and mentee will need to be on the same page regarding their values and principles to enjoy a successful relationship. Without establishing them first, a value clash later may cause feelings that can obstruct both sides from continuing effectively.

Having a sense of commonality, understanding each other's values, principles, strengths, and weaknesses will help make or break your relationship. Integrity, mutual respect, openness, trust, and active listening are shared values that should affect all your conversations.

Listening to a person's words isn't never enough. To understand their true intent, you must pay close attention to their body language, facial expressions, and emotions.

Strategy #3: Plan To Define Roles And Responsibilities

A learning environment requires tapping into what the mentee wants to learn, not what the mentor wants to teach, their roles, and responsibilities. Mentee need to put themselves in the driver's seat by setting realistic goals they wish to achieve with the help of their mentor. They should develop a plan listing short- and long-term goals and agree on a timeline to achieve them.

It may take more than one interaction to achieve the desired result. Mentors and mentee must hold each other accountable for turning failures and setbacks into learning opportunities.

Answering the following questions will help establish clear roles and responsibilities and basic guidelines for working together:

Who will do the preparation work?
What should be included?
How should the problem be formulated?
What information is needed to support or refute an idea?
In what way will solutions be implemented?
What is the best way to share learnings?
How should new ideas be prioritized?

Strategy #4: Work Together To Achieve Results

Act. A great plan is of no use without putting it into action.

Establish a logical agenda and hold yourselves and each other accountable to be prepared for a productive discussion based on the roles and responsibilities previously agreed to. Be receptive to each other's ideas, collaborate on brainstorming, and being open to another's suggestions.

Explore beyond your self-imposed limitations and shift your brain from a normal way of thinking to one that will provide you with answers in order to move forward using the first principles of thinking.

Determine a timeline for implementing, learning, sharing, reviewing, and determining the next steps.

A mentor should adopt a positive style in order to make a positive impact. When collaborating with your mentee, follow these tips:

-   Appreciate your mentee even when they make small progress.

119

- Don't be afraid to share critical feedback. If it's small, don't ignore it.
- Analyze the behavior and the choices. Never criticize the person.
- Encourage them to do more and better.

There Is No Greater Reward Than The Journey Itself

Relationships between mentors and mentee do not end when mentee reach their objectives. People form deep bonds that can last for a lifetime.

The mentor-mentee relationship remains with people for the rest of their lives. When dealing with challenging situations, they draw inspiration from their examples when speaking to others. The journey is what they will always remember, regardless of their paths.

Tips For Cultivating Relationships Within Your Community

The ability to build and maintain strong relationships is one of the most important characteristics of a community leader.

There are many people in the communities that we serve that would be happy to lend their time, talent, and resources to improve programs if they had the opportunity. Here are some tips to cultivate relationships and make connections in the community.

Close your eyes and think of five people whose influence has been most significant in your life….

Finding a way to connect with people can be intimidating, whether you're trying to establish a relationship socially, build connections for work, or make a great first impression. However, if you focus on showing that you really care about the person you're talking to, make some meaningful conversation, or work on making people feel comfortable, then you'll be on your way connecting with people you never thought of.

Through both formal and informal mentoring relationships over the years, I have been able to identify and set measurable goals, experience personal growth, and leadership skills. I have also been involved in more structured mentoring programs, as well as meaningful one-on-one relationships. A mentor-ship program is a terrific way to gain insight into your own goals and business practices by establishing accountability, building your professional network, and by gaining valuable experience.

There are several parameters that should be considered when building an effective mentor-ship relationship.

The bonds forged between mentors and mentee often extend into lifelong friendships.
A mentor-ship program can contribute to both business growth and new job creation in a similar way to entrepreneurial fulfillment programs.
Leadership is an advanced skill set, and mentor-ship will enhance it.

You Have to Build Relationships Over Time

A significant amount of time and effort goes into every relationship, whether personal or professional. We invest both time and money. Those of you who are already great at building relationships know that the process doesn't end when you collect business cards. It is a never-ending process. Keeping up with it requires constant attention. If you're still a bit shy, follow these tips to build relationships that will benefit both parties if they are nurtured.

Actively Listen

Whenever you meet someone for the first time or at a networking event, let them speak first. Ask insightful questions that will get them talking. Take notice of non-verbal cues and listen closely. Whenever they discuss something that bothers them, they cross their arms as a non-verbal cue. When recalling an especially exciting story, they may smile more than usual.

Getting people to tell their stories will help you endear yourself to them since they need to feel like a member of a larger group.

Document What You Do

Keep a pen on hand every time you talk to a new contact and jot down key details. Keep specific information about the person for future reference. Make sure to keep detailed notes if the person provides you with their birth date. Jot down how many children they have, their favorite book, or something they are passionate about. You will be able to use this information at some point in the future to express your gratefulness for something he/she has done for you.

Add Value

We all live hectic lives, working the majority of the week to ensure we follow up with new contacts regularly. Whenever you read an interesting story, receive a valuable email, or hear about a job opening, forward it to yourself with a short note. The information and thought you put into it will make a world of difference when building your relationship.

Show Your Appreciation

Learning to be grateful is a great way of showing appreciation. It seems to me that many people in our society go through life feeling entitled to anything they ask for. If you want to achieve your goals, you must work hard. Make sure to go above and beyond in showing appreciation when you receive a helpful hint or gift from a relationship. Knowing you have done someone a favor and they appreciate it. I know it's one of the best feelings in the world. Don't forget to convey that feeling to your new contact. Gratitude can be expressed in different ways. You should take the time to do it well.

See Between The Lines

Take a close look at your contacts, experiences, and mistakes as you continue to build the relationship. By learning from their experiences, you will not waste time doing the same thing again. Your goals will be achieved faster. On the other hand, you should also share your lessons learned with your acquaintances so that they can advance in their careers as well. It allows organizations to achieve their objectives faster by collaborating, sharing resources, and working together.

Possess the Right Motives

A foundation of trust underpins the relationships you build. Building a trusting relationship can take months or even years. A single mistake can ruin the relationship in seconds and destroy all trust. If your motives are not the right ones, and you are not operating with upstanding behavior, you are not doing what is right for the entire community. If you want to make yourself look good, gain media exposure, or serve your ego, you cannot focus on the other person. Foster relationships with the intention of seeing them flourish.

Take a proactive approach

Taking care of your relationships will help the foundation of your success in the future which applies to many aspects of your life. You cannot achieve wealth, emotionally or financially, without the help of those around you. Be confident in yourself and believe that the value you bring to the world will sincerely help those who want it. Exude confidence when anticipating others' needs. If you are reading LinkedIn and see that a new contact of yours has just taken a new position, send them a note congratulating them on their achievement. But don't stop there. If you know of a great book in that field, buy it and send it to them without announcing it. Being confident in your actions and giving more than you receive will bring you immense emotional joy.

Consider utilizing the above steps when building meaningful relationships to make the time spent more rewarding. Money and material possessions cannot measure your quality of life. It's not measured by the number of your relationships (although having a larger circle of influencers can't hurt). Whether you believe it or not, I would rather be lived in a life filled with lasting relationships and successful rather than a life filled with cars, houses, and vacations...and no one to share them with.

"Surround yourself with people who are going to lift you higher."

~Oprah Winfrey

Chapter 10
Planning for the Future is Never Too Late:
Don't Give Up

No more excuses. It's never too late to create the life that you want.

Do not be held back by the opinions of others or your past. Go after what you truly want regardless of the opinions of others. "Steer yourself in the direction of your dreams. You are the captain of your ship."

A new path to success can be started at any time. Putting in the work every day will allow you to mold your life the way you want it to be.

It's Never Too Late

Many people live unfulfilled lives. It is common for people to say they feel trapped by their responsibilities, lost, isolated, and demotivated. As a result, they believe that overcoming the challenges they face is impossible. People face debt, stress, a lack of direction as well as fear of failure and self-doubt. There is no end to this list.

They are more concerned with surviving each day and doing what they must just to remain alive. We often put off opportunities and experiences because we feel there are more reasons NOT to do things than to do them, even if we crave change in our lives. Often, we believe that we've left it too late to bring about the changes we crave.

When this happens, we curtail our dreams. We like to think that we are practical and pragmatic, but the truth is that we are afraid. Plain and simple: we are scared of taking a risk and failing.

The fact is that it's never too late to change your life and be who you want to be. Of course, people will always quote seemingly legitimate reasons, but if the desire is strong enough, there are no barriers that we cannot overcome.

Identify and dissect some of the most significant misconceptions:

It's too late to change because: "I'm too old." Many people set life goals based on their age. This custom is ridiculously old-fashioned, and it must perish. *"I want babies by X, a house by Y, and the mortgage paid off by Z."* The idea of attaching life goals to milestones is beneficial, of course. Despite this, the world has changed dramatically, and this old-fashioned view of personal achievement targets at socially accepted life points is now at odds with modern society.

Life doesn't have to be measured by it, and it shouldn't constrain you. It doesn't have to define who you are or prevent you from living the life of your dreams unless you allow it to be.

It is only when you are deceased that it is too late to change.

The world is filled with people of all ages altering their lives for the better. Ever wondered about the people in a room while taking a course during the night or at the university?

This image here shows you can always start something new no matter how late it is. You can accomplish your goals at any milestone in your life.

It's too late to change because: "Financial commitments trap me."

There is sometimes an element of fear associated with financial situations. When it comes to money, people feel emotional and past experiences greatly influence their outlook. There is a good chance that if you've experienced financial hardship at some point in your life, it has profoundly impacted your attitude toward wealth. Because we think we don't have enough money, we live with a restricted mindset about money. This makes us fear it. It's a dream of most of us to feel secure to have sufficient savings in the bank to go to bed soundly at night.

When we have a skewed mindset towards money, we can act emotionally and irrationally toward it. Occasionally, even when you know that you can't afford it, you purchase something just to make yourself feel better? What are your habits when it comes to saving money for a rainy

125

day? Would you consider yourself as one of those people who bury their heads in the sand to avoid thinking about it? As humans, we perceive power and money to be synonymous. Our tendency is to compare ourselves with others which can leave us feeling jealous and defeated.

Money-Centered Mindset

As a society, our relationship with money is deeply ingrained and seldom questioned. However, everyone can benefit from a bit of reflection in this regard because it is possible to feel differently about our financial existence. Changing your attitude towards money can have a profound impact on the way that you live your life.

It is common for people to say, in some form or another, that they don't have enough money. We experience a dramatic impact on our daily lives because of this limiting belief. Often, without our conscious awareness, our actions - or lack of actions - are dictated by such a mindset.

The revelation is that our beliefs are often not accurate indicators of how we are doing financially. Our over-anxious mind is protecting us instead. In addition, what is "enough" is generally interpreted and measured in lots of ways.

It takes time and effort to change your attitude toward money. Don't just disregard your desire for change because you cannot afford it when you have a deep desire to do so. You never know what will come your way. Be honest with yourself and think deeply before you make a decision.

Ask Yourself

What is more important: happiness or wealth?
How brutal can you be with yourself?
How far can you stretch your budget so that you can save more or pay off debts?
What emotional spending can you cut out?

It's too late to change because: "I don't have time."

When you make that pledge, *"Yeah, I'll be there!"* Pat yourself on the back, and you'll feel better right away. Intoxicating and compelling is the strategy of starting tomorrow. The moment you commit, you immediately feel more optimistic about taking action on something you've been dreading, tackling jobs you don't want to do. Do you recognize this?

Procrastination is simply another name for this strategy. In other words, it's a way to feel better about not doing something. Is this the answer? No.

Start Now!

If you want to change your life, you must start making small yet effective changes as soon as possible. Someone once said, *"The definition of insanity is doing the same thing over and over again and expecting a different result."* While this quote is usually attributed to Albert Einstein, there is little substantial proof that he ever said or wrote anything of that sort. However, irrespective of who said it, it is a very powerful statement to live by.

Now is the right time. There will never be a time to act, so we fool ourselves into believing it's not feasible or practical. Fear is speaking subconsciously here. As far as solutions go, facing the facts is the only way out. Decide how important it is for you to prioritize your wants and needs. In order to make those changes, you need to look for the time to do so. Leaving it for too long will make it harder. The dream cannot be transformed into reality unless you grow accustomed to it.

Taking an honest look at how you use your time is a good place to start. It might be necessary to let go of some things in order to make time for making the changes that you desire.

The key to getting your desired destination is to get started and do something about it now. You can't get anything done if you continue to wait until *'tomorrow.'*

When You Stop Dreaming and Stop Pursuing Your Goals, You Stop Being YOU.

It is better to work towards your goals than to drift further away from them or to allow them to disappear as if they never existed. By losing or giving up on your dreams and goals, you are giving up on yourself. You will lose yourself by giving up on yourself.

I'm not ready to give up on myself! Aside from that, I refuse to abandon my goals and aspirations for the future. *How about you? What are your plans?*

It's Never too Late to Change Your Life and Live Differently....

Change is something that some of us look forward to, while others push it aside to avoid them.

To answer this question, I believe we must honestly ask ourselves - how often don't we let ourselves experience new opportunities or life experiences, or even give up certain dreams because we're using the oldest excuse in the book? How often do we cross things off our bucket list not because we've accomplished them but because we're too fixated on our inability or incapacity to accomplish them?

When you do something just once, it's already too much.

Willpower is the most powerful force, and it is the power to look beyond the obstacles in front of you, overcoming them, or walking away from them, not because you can't complete it, but because plans change.

Changing plans is a normal part of life. There is never a wrong time to make a change.

"I'll Start Tomorrow."

By pushing your personal goals to the side, you are subconsciously letting your brain know that it's not important. Your goals are always important and valuable.

Identify the habit or place where you are spending the most time that is preventing you from moving forward with your goals:
- Is saying yes to everything and taking on other people's projects is more important to you than your own?
- Are you burnt out?
- Can't figure out where to start because you feel overwhelmed?

It's Never Too Late to Plan Your Career: What Are You Going to Do Next Year?

You can never start planning your career too late.

You can start today and move toward an exciting career path even if you were never in a planning mode before, and especially if you don't like your current job.

Vacation plans are usually more passionate than career plans for most people. Perhaps they don't know how, or it's too difficult for them to think about the future and the uncertainties it brings. It might be difficult to decide what appeals to you, and you may not know what to do if you have a vague idea of where you want to be in a decade.

The Journey of Life is Full of Ups and Downs: Don't Give Up

Successes and failures are part of life. Throughout the dance, there are highs, lows, and everything in-between. To me, nature is the best teacher in our lives and a great example to follow. There is a time for sowing and a time for reaping. It takes time between wanting and having a baby. People accept this as normal; they don't question it. It's a law!

What is it about life that causes so many of us to call it a day during challenges? When we grasp an understanding of this law of life, it is a strong reminder that things require effort and time. Things do not happen overnight. Continue to move forward and don't give up.

Giving up Makes the Situation Worse

Often, people feel like giving up because they believe that the pain will go away or by giving up something will shift for the better. This is true on many levels.

There is a difference between giving up on a long project in school and giving up on life as a whole. Or maybe not for everyone. (If you are experiencing such feelings, I urge you to seek professional help). So why will giving up make things worse? We believe that growth gives us strength and gives us the belief that our future is brighter. Giving up is not what we want most; it is taking the easy route. It gives us temporary relief, but the future is painful. Our growth gives us confidence that our future is brighter.

When Giving Up Is Okay

If you are truly unhappy with something in your life, then you should be perfectly okay with quitting. Giving up is never okay, in my opinion. However, if you are truly unhappy about what you are doing, then you should give up on that particular project and find another project that interest you.

In other words, you don't just give up on something because it's difficult or challenging; you quit something you genuinely don't want to pursue.

You are the Creator of Your Own Life

Taking charge of your life is the road to success. Remember that you decide what you want, what things mean to you, and how you want to live your life. The creator of your own life is you. You decide what you want, what matters to you, and how you live your life.

Don't let anything hold you back from living your life to the fullest!

Don't Give Up On Yourself...You Are Stronger Than You Think

Whenever life gets overwhelming, giving up may seem like the easy thing to do. However, nobody will benefit from your gifts if you don't. So don't give up on yourself when you face hardship. You are better than you think. This is not the end. It's the beginning of something wonderful. If, at first, you don't succeed, keep trying until you succeed. Are you ready to become the person that you always dreamed of becoming? Absolutely!

Don't Give Up on Yourself

Do you love yourself? Some people look for the easy way out when life gets tough. Consequently, they are never able to fulfill their goals and dreams in life. Avoid falling into this trap. We as humans are wired to avoid pain and seek happiness. Most of us will choose to take shortcuts when given the choice. Sadly, success does not come easy. It takes a lot of hard work, dedication, and focus for something to be valuable to achieve.

You have to work hard to change your life. During the process of becoming a new version of yourself, you will doubt yourself at times. Tough times aren't meant to consume you, however. Rather than seeing them as obstacles, consider them as opportunities.

A few privileged individuals are not able to achieve greatness. Instead, it is something everyone possesses. When a way cannot be found, make one yourself. This philosophy has served me well throughout my life. However, if you aren't willing to make an effort and do what needs to be done, you will be forced into giving up. Is that what you want? I'm going to guess no. There is no right or wrong answer here; you must decide for yourself.

Here are reasons you shouldn't give up on yourself, even when you feel like giving up:

1. Failure Is A Part Of Life:

A successful life cannot be achieved without experiencing failure. I get it, failing sucks. When you invest your time, money, belief, faith, and energy into something that doesn't work out, it's easy to feel defeated. The problem is that society frowns upon defeat. Failing is viewed as something to avoid at all costs.

Don't waste your time trying to resist failure if you believe that your intellect, hard work, and passion can protect you. Life is full of failures.

It is inevitable that everyone will fail at some point in their lives. Almost every successful individual in the world has failed, including me. Don't be afraid to fail next time and remember that it's an opportunity for you to grow as individuals and learn from failures.

Success is yours for when you know how to turn failure into opportunity.

2. Achieving Success Is Closer Than You Think:

Whenever something doesn't work out, it is easy to lose enthusiasm. This is usually when negative thoughts show up, and you start to think that things will never get better. If you aren't careful, you will start believing these things to be true. As a result, you may give up altogether.

We don't realize that we are close to achieving success until it's too late. My biggest breakthroughs in life have occurred at the moment when I felt like quitting. If you work hard and believe in yourself, you will achieve your goals without a question ask.

Waiting patiently and willingly will help you get the answer you've been looking for. This is why giving up is not an option for you. When you feel like the intensity is increasing, you're getting closer to your goal!

I can't let you back down now. Take action, keep growing, and keep believing. *You can shift your thinking from "I can't do this" to "I must do this" when you learn to view your struggles as opportunities to grow stronger, better, and wiser. Don't give up on it.*

3. The World Needs You And Your Gifts:

Many people become enraptured in other people's dreams. In their desire to be seen and validated, they dim their own light in the process. Did you know that you have amazing gifts that the world is waiting for? Maybe these gifts are lying dormant inside of you because you are too afraid to share them.

The realization is living your passion and sharing your gifts may result in a happier and more fulfilling life. Serving others and adding value to their lives is part of your unique capacity. You have extraordinary talents and gifts that there are people out there who need. Your purpose is what drives you.

If you don't know what your purpose is, don't stop looking. However, for others, it takes longer, and that is okay. Nobody is expecting you to be successful overnight, and neither should you.

You've got one life to live, and it's your job to make it something beautiful. This is why you need to create a life that you love. Honoring your truth is one of the most selfless things that you can do for yourself.

4. Anything Is Possible for You:

People who start out with nothing can become successful in this world. Despite their circumstances, they were still able to achieve great feats in life. Why? Because they had the belief that anything was possible. Whatever you are striving for in life, I promise you that there is someone in the world who has already achieved it.

Reality is something you create. You will only encounter limitations if you believe there are limits to what you can achieve in life. Because of this, when things get tough, you will always want to give up. On the other hand, someone who believes the world is their oyster will try anything and everything. Risking all to obtain all is what they are willing to do. Are you willing to?

For just one week, tell yourself you are a champion instead of listening to yourself like a victim if you struggle with self-confidence. That's the advice of best-selling author Jon Gordon. *The results will blow you away." I guarantee you"*.

You Are Stronger Than You Thought

Let's take a moment to consider how far we've come. You are strong now. Could you have gotten where you are without it? That's impossible. Celebrate yourself and your accomplishments instead of being your worst critic. Rather than looking for reasons for their lack of success, many people find reasons why they shouldn't be successful. As a result, they experience barriers to success in life.

I never dealt with anything in my life that I couldn't handle. Mental strength was not something I achieved by thinking. Rather, I had to exercise it every single day as if it were a muscle. Consequently, I became more adept at approaching challenges positively. Since I was a child, I had no doubts that I could overcome anything.

Various experiences and challenges develop attitudes, cognitions, emotions, and personal values that make up mental toughness. Quality of life is determined by the strength of your mind. Don't give up the next time life throws you a curve-ball. Don't give up on yourself. It is entirely possible for you to do more than you ever dreamed possible. You must believe it but most of all believe in yourself.

5. Regret Is The Worst:

What are you doing right now that will enable your success? If you can't answer this question with a detailed answer, now is the time to change that. One of the hardest things to do in life is live life with regrets. You don't want to look back and wish that you had made different decisions, do you? Even if things turn out badly, people are more likely to regret not doing it.

Giving up dreams can be an option for someone. Success in life requires you to be responsible for yourself. If you don't want to live with regrets, don't make excuses and start making progress. Focus on moving forward rather than dwelling on what *"could have been"*.

Learn from your mistakes, embrace them. As a result of the experiences you have had, you have become the person you are now. It's not worth regretting. To reach your emotional threshold and say, "I am ready for something new," you must experience pain, fear, lack of motivation, and confusion at times. Live in alignment with your truth and trust that everything will unfold in your existence exactly as it should.

Giving Up Is The Worst Mistake You Can Ever Make

From time to time, you may need a simple reminder of what your life's purpose is. Take these 6 reasons into consideration the next time you struggle with motivation and want to give up.

1. Having dreams may take a long time, and that's okay.
2. Never give up. You must be willing to taste defeat in order to experience success. Those who are most successful in this world never gave up.
3. Choose *today* to be the best version of yourself.
4. A single decision could lead to a life-changing experience. You must always get back up when you fall.
5. Don't let going of your faith cause you to lose it.
6. Your strength exceeds your expectations. You must believe it, feel it, embrace it, and own it. It's yours already!

Why Do I Feel Like Giving Up?

The struggles you experience in life can leave you feeling overwhelmed, leading to a desire to throw in the towel. Living in a complex world can be exhausting. You may be suffering from a depressive episode, or you may have lost a loved one. Maybe you are dealing with the pain of divorce or separation.

Throughout our lives, we experience a number of distressing events. The fact that there are also joyous moments in our lives can be hard to remember during trying times. The darkness may blind you, but there is still hope. Telling your family and friends that you are struggling is one action you can take. When you're depressed, it's hard to do this. You are loved by your loved ones, and they care about your well-being. You may want to reach out to someone close to you and ask for help. Your support network may also be able to assist you, as well as a licensed mental health professional.

When you suffer from depression or have trouble enjoying life, therapy can make a big difference. An individual who has difficulty finding joy in life may be emotionally drained to the point you are exhausted, but counseling will help if you get it sooner than later.

It can sometimes be a struggle just to get by. People who feel this way need to get help, find direction, and have a purpose in life.

Do You Feel Like Giving Up?

Sometimes life isn't as easy as it seems. Many of us have experienced hardships. Some days are downright depressing and even miserable. But, despite this, life happens for us, not to us. Nevertheless, when the desire to give up strikes, what should you do? It's our choices, not our conditions, that ultimately shape the quality of our lives.

According to another great leader, Theodore Roosevelt, *"The best things in life will not be handed to you without effort, pain, and difficulty."* Nothing in the world is worth having or doing unless you work hard for them. Your goal should be to earn them back.

What to do when you feel like giving up?

The good news is that you can take concrete steps to change your state right now. Regardless of what your goals are, you can retrain your mind to reach them. When you feel like giving up. STOP – Breathe – Inhale – Exhale and remind yourself...I am here for a reason.

My life has been filled with failure after failure after failure.
I succeed because of that.

~Anonymous

Despite the pain, there will be times when it seems like giving up is the only way out. You can't win if you give up, so keep fighting.

When you give your best, your dreams will come true.
Success is yours. Make your dreams a reality; it's your turn.

This inspirational quote about the power of never giving up will fill your day with energy and passion. You must be willing to take on all challenges in life and never give up on them. Many great people have succeeded in life by never giving up at all.

Having a *never give up* attitude will allow you to succeed in life despite adverse circumstances, even if they may come across difficulties in your life. Successful people who have overcome many difficulties have achieved stardom and popularity no matter what the circumstances are.

Solid Reasons Why You Should Never Give Up

As life changes, circumstances change - sometimes your circumstances are good, other times they are average, and sometimes they are harsh or difficult. People you know - friends, colleagues, relatives - also often change.

Throughout our lives, we may face a variety of difficult situations that force us to consider *giving up.*

Sometimes we give up way too soon and just as we are about to make this massive breakthrough to success. We quit even before we have begun the new activity. We quit just before reaching this amazing breakthrough to success. The mind will always feel like enough is enough, and how much more effort it would take to succeed. Don't give up beforehand under the pressure of your silly feelings!

Life sometimes provides certain things that you cannot change so better accept them and still find a way to move forward. There are times you can't change certain circumstances or situations.

You have only two choices, either to give up or to keep going. Asking *"Why me?"* will never be answered because there is no answer to this question if you are a go-getter.

Are You Used To Facing Challenges?
Each day is a challenge whether you realize it or not. Most of the times, the challenges are rather simple and manageable.

A challenge keeps us active, smart and in shape. The correct response to a challenge is to turn it around and take it on. Every successful person has done so, and you can too. In addition to making sure that you are pushing yourself in the right direction, that also motivates others around you if you are heading a team, department, or organization. But you are stronger than you think you are. Whatever you think, whatever emotion you feel, you will put yourself behind it with strength.

By exaggerating your inability to cope, you may overestimate the stress of work or the process. As a result, you may waste time and energy dreading going to work and complain about difficulties at home.

Having learned about the self-defeating process, you should convince yourself that you are stronger than you think. You have the strength to accomplish any goal you set for yourself. One or two failures is no barrier in accomplishing your goals. What would you give up for your dreams?

You Have To Struggle To Reach To The Top!
To succeed, you must push yourself. No extraordinary results can be accomplished unless you challenge yourself. Whether it is sports or finance or scientific research, the extraordinary results won't just show up out of nowhere. To achieve extraordinary things, you have to break out of your comfort zone. Therefore, do not consider quitting just because you don't want to be uncomfortable. The greatest achievements in life are
137

often achieved outside of your comfort zone. Throwing up your hands and giving up won't get you there.

Don't Quit on Yourself

Quitting every time, you face a new challenge can become a self-destructive habit. Your perception of yourself might change. Because you can't seem to fight with difficulties long enough to see positive results, you may begin to believe you're weak or a failure.

The good news is that you can change it completely. Prove to yourself that you're strong enough to tolerate more than you think: Just because you feel challenged doesn't mean you should give up right away.

What are you trying to achieve now? What has anyone else succeeded at before? There is always someone in the world who has accomplished what you want to achieve so whatever your goal is - *it can be achieved!*

Remember that you are capable of doing anything if someone else is. Don't give up no matter what!

You Deserve to be Happy

Have faith that you deserve to be happy and successful. Happiness and success are the rights of all people. Be persistent in your efforts until you achieve your goals and keep a positive attitude. Regardless of what anyone tells you, stay true to yourself.

Yet, we all struggle, and perhaps your current set of circumstances are the toughest. Now is not the time to lose sight of the fact that life is complicated. Balancing work, home, and family can be a challenge. During all the busyness of everyday life, you deserve to find a little happiness. Take action to prevent these small speed bumps on the road from ruining your day.

Stop procrastinating and start living! It is never too late.
Find the time to make your dreams and goals come true by not giving up
on them.

~Dr. Christina S. Rogers

Success Framework Assessment Model:
The 6Cs to Success

Based on the 6Cs to Success framework assessment model, I have developed a set of guiding principles for achieving my goals. These are my guiding principles for achieving success in my life.

The 6Cs of Success Framework Assessment Model

Clarity (C1)	Confidence (C2)	Commitment (C3)	Concentration (C4)	Communication (C5)	Completion (C6)

Self-Check Assessment to Complete for Yourself

Answer the following questions below. Take about 5 minutes to go through each question and mark the number that applies to you, "0" represents the lowest self-score number and "10" represents the highest self-score number.

(C1) Clarity

I have a clear vision of what I am pursuing in life to attain my goals.

1	2	3	4	5	6	7	8	9	10

(C2) Confidence

I am confident in my ability to attain my current goals successfully.

1	2	3	4	5	6	7	8	9	10

(C3) Commitment

I give 100% of my commitment to aim for success and pursue a better life for myself.

1	2	3	4	5	6	7	8	9	10

(C4) Concentration

I have the mindset and strength to thrive for success and focus on the next step. I need to reach my goals.

1	2	3	4	5	6	7	8	9	10

(C5) Communication

Communication have played an important factor in my leadership skills to network with people to guide me in the right direction.

1	2	3	4	5	6	7	8	9	10

(C6) Completion

I have accomplished my goals.

1	2	3	4	5	6	7	8	9	10

Grading yourself on the Self-Check Assessment Evaluation:

It's time for results!

Add up all your self-scores on this checklist and write down your current total.

Self-Score Total: _____

If your self-score is over "40", then you're in pretty good shape in the recent stages of your journey to success. Keep up the good work and build on your accomplishments.
If your self-score is under "40", you should very seriously rethink the goals you are pursuing and how you are working towards them. You must put in a little more work towards accomplishing your goals.

Life should always involve a process of self-evaluation and self-correction, self-knowledge, and self-mastery. Repeat this self-check assessment regularly, act on the information you generate, and you will move progressively more in the direction of achieving all that you are here on this earth to do!

Thank you for taking the 6Cs Success Framework Assessment Model. I appreciate your hard work! In this section, you will discuss your scores in each category and what each category means to you in your day-to-day life. Your results should be shared with the most important people in your life. Don't forget to encourage them to take the assessment too. It can benefit all people in accomplishing their goals.

Knowing yourself is the beginning of life purpose

Remember that you can still be kind, loving and generous while protecting your energy and creating healthy boundaries. Those things aren't mutually exclusive to each other.

"I was always incredibly driven and found it impossible to relax. I felt that if I slacked off for a minute to enjoy myself, then so many things would be missed."

~Sandra Bullock

Final Thoughts

Success comes from YOU. Success comes from creating the best life for yourself. Apart from this, it's *never* too late. Of course, life is hard and filled with complexities. It's challenging and stressful, and we all have been there and done that. However, it is most often our limiting beliefs and perceptions that make things appear harder than they are. Out subconscious does a great job of looking after us, but if we're not careful, it can also restrict us. Too many people still hold outdated opinions about age and wealth. We live only once. To truly experience the magic of life and to achieve our dreams, we have to ensure that we make the most of every opportunity that life throws our way. We need to ensure that we prioritize what is important to us, work through our limiting beliefs, and take action. You are in full control of your life. Make sure that you don't look back with regrets.

Many people continue to wonder, what's the difference between a boss and a leader. Well based on my personal experience, as a leader, you lead, as a boss, you drive. A boss will teach you what to do. Leaders will show you why a particular action is necessary and how. Those who inspire others to dream bigger, learn better, do better, and become better are leaders. Life is all about having more than you need.

You can never have enough if you focus on what you don't have in life. If you are willing to pursue your dreams, they can all come true. It doesn't matter what obstacles you face. Keep going if you hit a wall or give up when you encounter one. Decide whether to go around it, climb it, or go through it. Personal excellence requires self-evaluation in order to uncover your strengths, weaknesses, attitudes and emotions, life principles, and beliefs. A key aspect of personal excellence is identifying and establishing your career and life goals after deciding what your strengths and weaknesses are. Remember, success comes from you and only you...no one else. Continue to put in the work and doors will open for you sooner than you think.

Just believe in yourself – *You can do it!*

Dr. Christina S. Rogers

Made in the USA
Las Vegas, NV
25 September 2022